PROJECT ENGINEER: Lyman Coleman, Serendipity House

WRITER FOR NOTES/COMMENTARY: Richard Peace, Gordon Conwell Seminary.

CONTRIBUTORS: Denny Rydberg, University Presbyterian Church, Seattle □ Gordon Fee, Gordon Conwell Seminary, Boston □ Virginia Zachert, Medical College of Georgia, Augusta □ Janet Kobobel, Zondervan Publishing House, Grand Rapids □ Peter Menconi, Professional Consultants, Denver □ John Mallison, Board of Education, Uniting Church in Australia, Sydney □ John U'Ren, Scripture Union, Melbourne □ Ken Anderson, Synod of South Australia, Uniting Church of Australia, Adelaide □ Anton Baumohl, Scripture Union, Bristol, England □ Lance Pierson, Freelance writer, London □ Emlyn Williams, Scripture Union, Cambridge, England.

PUBLISHER: Serendipity House is a resource community specializing in the equipping of pastors and church leaders for small group ministry in the local church in the English speaking world. A list of training events and resources can be obtained by writing one of the addresses below.

SERENDIPITY U.S.A.
Serendipity House
Box 1012
Littleton, Colorado 80160

Telephone: 800-525-9563

96 97 98 99 / CHG / 10 9 8 7 6 5 4 3 2

Copyright: © 1988, Serendipity Foundation. All rights reserved. Printed in U.S.A.

1 CORINTHIANS

LYMAN COLE[MAN]

NF 225 COL
Coleman, Lyman
Study Guide for the Book of 1 Corinthians

MW01480460

PERSONAL EXCELLENCE THROUGH BIBLE STUDY

Mastering The Basics

PERSONAL EXCELLENCE THROUGH BIBLE STUDY

All Scripture is God-breathed
and is useful for teaching,
rebuking, correcting
and training in righteousness,
so that the man of God
may be thoroughly equipped
for every good work.

2 TIMOTHY 3:16-17 NIV

N. LONSDALE
UNITED CHURCH
LIBRARY

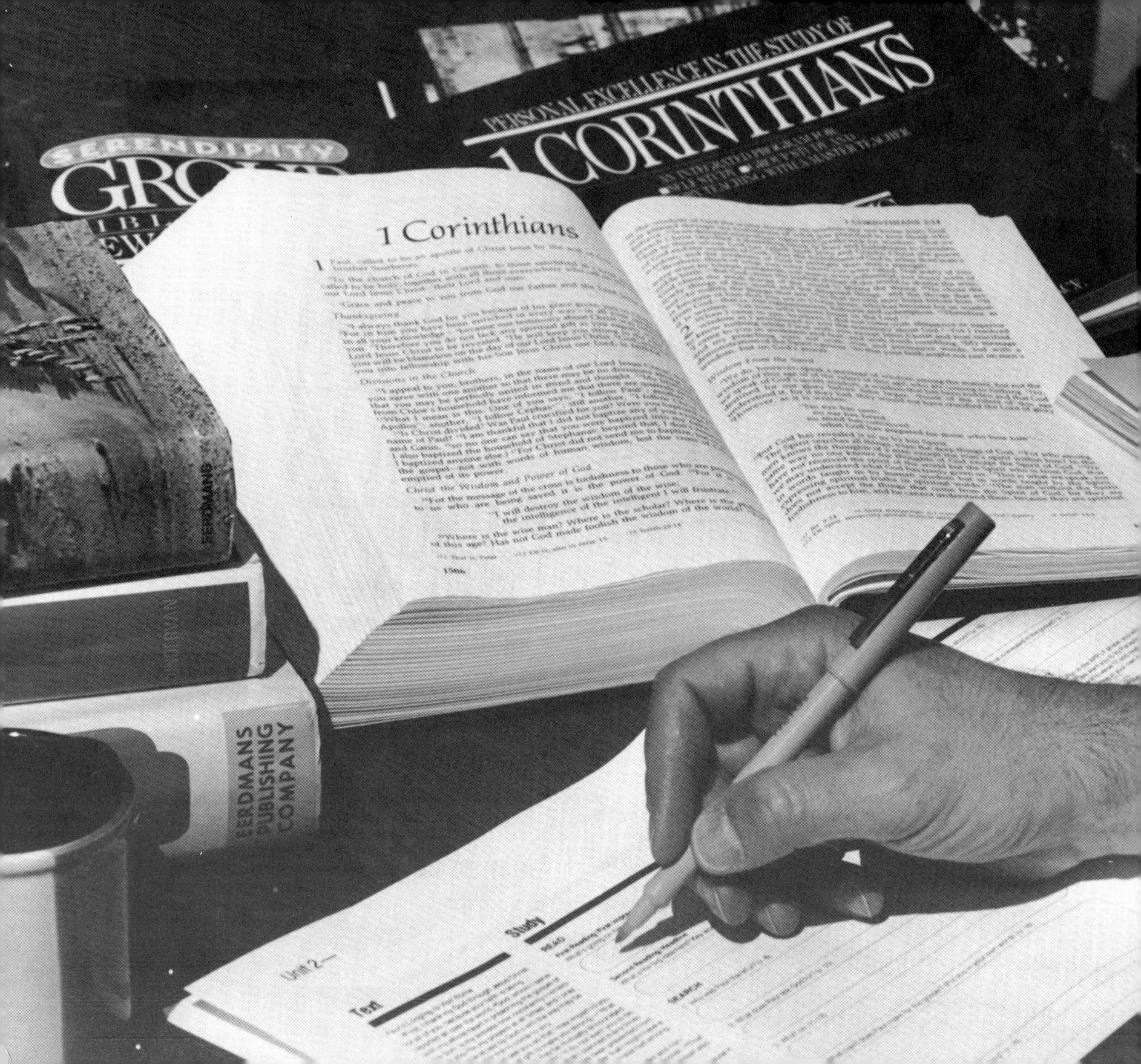
PERSONAL EXCELLENCE IN THE STUDY OF
1 CORINTHIANS
SERENDIPITY
1 Corinthians
Thanksgiving
Divisions in the Church
Christ the Wisdom and Power of God
Wisdom From the Spirit
1 CORINTHIANS 2:14
1506
EERDMANS
ZONDERVAN
EERDMANS PUBLISHING COMPANY
Unit 2—
Study
Text
READ

THREE PARTS TO THE PROGRAM: CHOOSE ONE, TWO, OR ALL THREE

Some like to travel alone. Some like to travel in groups. Some like to travel with a small group on a huge passenger liner with a tour guide and lectures along the way.

In this program you can do all three: (1) Self study—on your own, (2) Group study—with a small intimate group, or (3) Church-wide groups—with the pastor or associate minister providing exegetical teaching on the passage when all of the groups get together.

1. Self Study

Those who cannot be in a group can still do the home assigment and get in on the pastoral teaching of the Scripture passage after having completed the assignment, like a college course.

The Bible study assignment worksheets in this book are designed for lay-people who are beginners at Bible study. The study is inductive—that is, you do your own research and draw your own conclusions. If you don't know the meaning of key words, there is a glossary of terms and a running commentary on the page after the worksheet. The Scripture passage for study is printed next to the worksheet, so that you have all of the material you need to complete the study on your own. Each unit of study will take about 30 to 45 minutes to complete, or about 10 minutes a day.

There are three parts to each worksheet: (1) Read—to get the "bird's eye view" of the passage and jot down your first impressions, (2) Search—to get the "worm's eye view" of the passage—digging into the passage verse by verse with specific questions to look for and jot down, and (3) Apply—to find out what God is saying to you through this Scripture, using a different approach each time—self inventory, written prayer, goal setting, scripture memory, spiritual principles, practical project, etc.

The self study assignment is coordinated with the group study and the expository teaching from the pastor/teacher, giving you the option of supplementing your spiritual diet with two more forms of Bible study.

2. Group Study

The group approach is not only more fun, but also offers a far greater potential for interaction with the Scripture.

The group can be anything from 3 or 4 people, to 30 or 40 people meeting around card tables in the same house. By dividing into groups of 4, you allow not only for maximum participation, but also make room for new people to join the group without making the group too large for sharing.

The group can meet anytime, anywhere during the week: ☐ in homes ☐ offices ☐ restaurants ☐ at breakfast ☐ over coffee ☐ in the evening ☐ at the Sunday school hour just before the teaching session by the pastor/teacher.

The completed home study assignment becomes the basis for the group sharing experience. On the worksheet for each unit is a "Group Agenda" column with guided questions on three levels of sharing: (1) To Begin/10 Minutes, (2) To Go Deeper/20 Minutes, and (3) To Close/5 to 20 Minutes.

You can either have a trained leader for the group, or rotate the leadership around the group—each person taking the responsibility in turn. If you have more than 5 or 6 in the group and you divide into groups of 4 for sharing, you ask one person in each group to be the leader of the foursome. The leader

3. Expository Teaching for All Groups Together

This is the Queen Elizabeth II model—a luxury liner cruise with the whole church on board, and the pastor or associate offering in-depth teaching on the passage after the groups have met.

The teaching session can be open to anyone. In fact, a good way to get people interested in the Self Study and Group Study parts of the program is to start teaching the course at a popular church activity and invite groups to get together and join in.

The Pastor/Teacher Commentary corresponds unit by unit with the Self Study/Group Study Book, with suggestions on how to link what the student has studied and the group has discussed with the teaching session.

Further instructions are provided in the Pastor/Teacher Commentary.

simply looks over the questions in the "Group Agenda" column and chooses questions from the list for sharing.

In the Apply part of Unit One, the group is asked to discuss personal and corporate goals for the time together and agree on a common discipline: (1) to complete the Bible study home assignment before the group meets, (2) to attend the group meetings except in case of emergency, (3) to share in leading the group, (4) to keep anything that is shared in the group in confidence, (5) to reach out to others who are not in a group and invite them to fill the "empty chair", and (6) to attend the teaching session with the Pastor/Teacher.

The group lasts as long as the course lasts. If the group wishes to continue after the course is over, the group will have to decide on another course to study or come up with its own purpose and agenda.

Group Agenda

Divide into groups of 4 before starting on these questions. Follow the time recommendations.

TO BEGIN / 10 Minutes (Choose 1 or 2)

☐ Have you ever been to a Jewish bar mitzvah or wedding? ☐ How valuable was your own religious instruction in bringing you to Christ? ☐ What would you do differently about religious instruction for your kids? ☐ What did you jot down for READ? ☐ Who does Paul remind you of in this passage: a prosecuting attorney? a diplomat, a drill sergeant in the Marine Corps, etc.

TO GO DEEPER / 20 Minutes (Choose 2 or 3)

☐ Go around and answer the questions under SEARCH—one person answering question 1, the next person answering 2, etc. ☐ What's so radical about Paul's teaching here? ☐ Why was Paul so concerned about a minor thing like circumcision? ☐ What would Paul have to say about our Christian rituals and initiation rites today? ☐ Case History: Bob's grandfather was a country preacher; his father was a deacon; and Bob has been on the board of the church for twenty years. "If anybody deserves to go to heaven, it is Bob." Do you agree?

TO CLOSE / 5-20 Minutes (Choose 1 or 2)

QUESTIONS

About the Self Study

1. *What if you don't know anything about the Bible?* No problem. The home assignment worksheet is designed to lead you step by step in your study. And, there are Notes on the following page to give you help with key words, places and difficult passages.

2. *What do you mean by the inductive method of Bible study?* It is the scientific method applied to Bible study. You begin by observing facts and draw conclusions based on these facts, just like a scientific experiment.

3. *Why go to all of the trouble of doing your own study if you can find out what the passage really means when the pastor/teacher teaches it on Sunday?* There is no substitute for your own study. None.

About the Group Study

1. *How many do you need to start a group?* Four people, plus an empty chair.

2. *What is the "empty chair" for?* A reminder that there is always room for one more.

3. *What do you do when the group gets too large?* When the group reaches 8, you split into two groups of 4—4 at the kitchen table, and 4 at the dining table. When you reach 12, you add another card table, etc.

4. *What if you have someone in the group who likes to talk (too much)?* On the home assignment worksheet, there is a "Group Agenda" with questions for three levels of sharing: (a) to begin the session, (b) to go deeper, and (c) to close . . . with time limits for each phase. The questions will keep you on track if you follow them.

5. *Who is the leader?* In the first two or three sessions, someone who has been trained by the pastor. After that, you rotate the leadership around the group.

6. *Can you share a book with your wife?* No.

7. *If you run into a conflict that makes it impossible to attend the group meetings, can you stay in the self study part and attend the expository teaching session with the pastor?* Yes.

8. *What if you do not complete the home assignment before the group meeting?* You should still go to the group meeting. In fact, some groups have found it valuable to do their homework together after they get to the meeting.

About the Church-wide Teaching Session

1. *What if the pastor cannot possibly take on the teaching responsibility?* The pastor must be totally committed to this program for it to have maximum impact. If the pastor cannot do the teaching, the pastor should appoint someone else with teaching skills and considerable background in Scripture to do the teaching.

2. *Can people who are not in the self study or group study phases of this program still get in on the teaching session?* Yes.

3. *Can the teaching session be at the Sunday school hour or even the Sunday morning worship service?* Yes. In fact, this would be a good way to interest people in joining a group.

4. *Can the group study and the teaching session be at the same time?* Yes. In fact, this would be a great idea if you have the time and space for groups.

5. *Do you recommend a steady diet of this program?* No. You should take a vacation between courses and disband the groups. Then, when you start a new course, invite the groups to shuffle and reach out to new people.

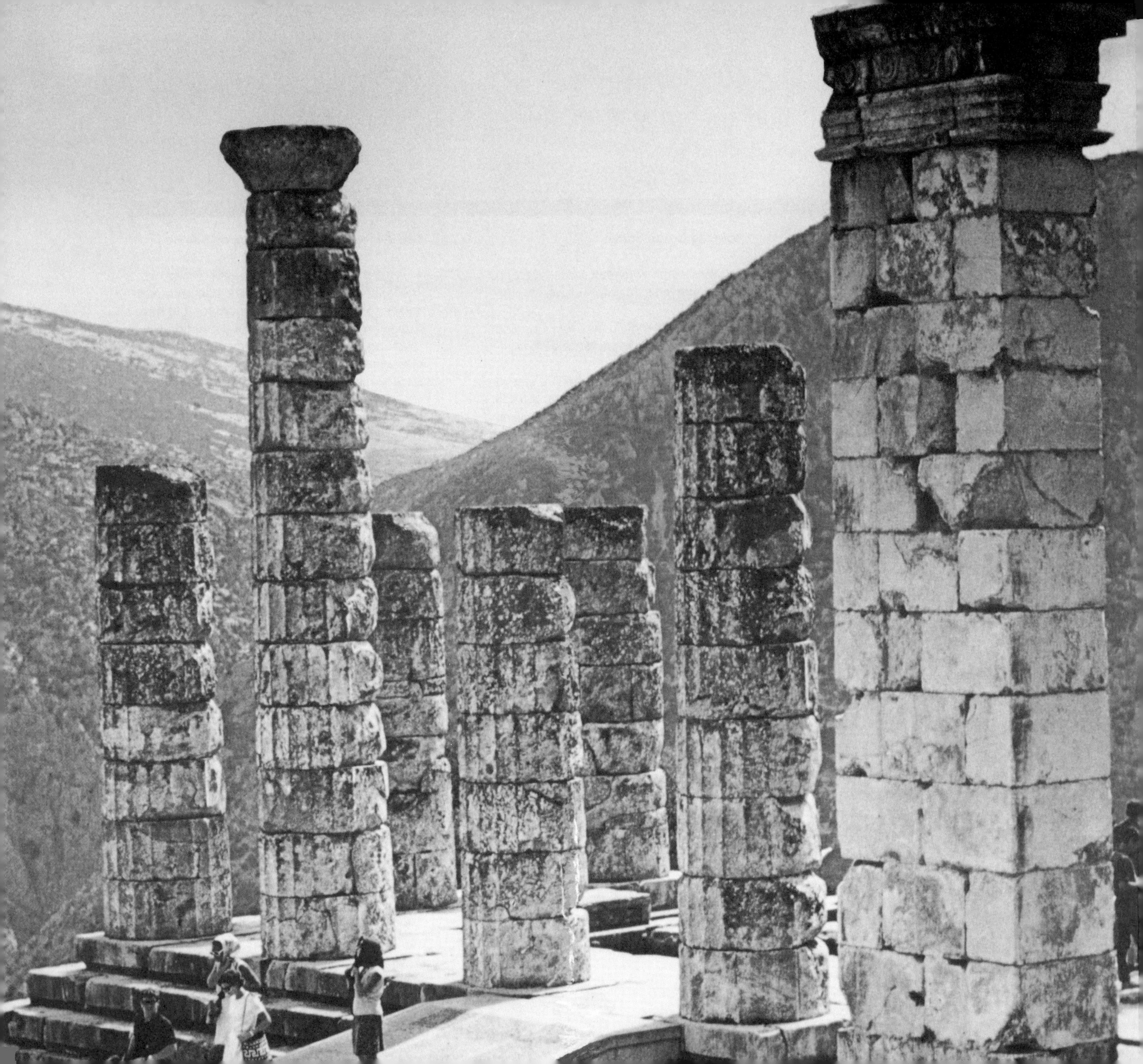

INTRODUCTION TO THE BOOK OF 1 CORINTHIANS

Corinth—The City
Corinth was an unusual city. After its capture by the Roman Legions in 146 B.C., the city was leveled to the ground and lay waste for nearly 100 years until Julius Caesar rebuilt it in 44 B.C. But then it grew rapidly—largely because of its unique geographical location. It lay at the neck of a narrow isthmus that connected the two parts of Greece. Thus it controlled all north-south land traffic. To the east and the west of the city were two fine harbors. Both goods and actual ships were hauled across the 4 mile wide Corinthian Isthmus. Thus Corinth also controlled the sea routes between east and west. All this added up to wealth and influence. By the time of Paul's visit some 100 years after its rebuilding, Corinth had become the capital of the province of Achaia and the third most important city in the Roman Empire—after Rome and Alexandria.

In this wealthy, young city excess seemed to be the norm. The city was stocked with art treasures purchased from around the Empire. It became a center of philosophy—though apparently few citizens were really interested in the serious study of philosophy, preferring rather stirring orations on the faddish topic of the moment delivered by the numerous itinerant philosophers that had been drawn to the city. Even in religion, the same excess was obvious. The Greek author Pausanius describes some 26 pagan shrines and temples including the great temples of Apollo and Aphrodite. In Old Corinth, a thousand temple prostitutes had served Aphrodite, the goddess of love, and New Corinth continued this tradition of sexual freedom. The city developed a world-wide reputation for vice and debauchery.

Luxury was the hallmark of Corinth. Because the storms in the Aegean Sea were so treacherous, sailors preferred to put into one of the harbors and transport their cargo to the other side by land—despite the exorbitant prices charged by the Corinthians. The result was that goods from around the world passed through its ports. This also meant that some 400,000 slaves were kept in Corinth to provide the labor for this arduous job.

Into this new city flowed people from around the Empire. There were "Greek adventurers and Roman bourgeois, with a tainting infusion of Phoenicians; a mass of Jews, ex-soldiers, philosophers, merchants, sailors, freed men, slaves, trades-people, hucksters and agents of every form of vice." (Farrar.) Rootless, proud, independent, egalitarian, individualistic, rich—together they shaped this new city into the cosmopolitan capital that it was in Paul's day. Not surprisingly, it was here that Paul had to fight the battle to prevent Christianity from succumbing to the debilitating enticements offered by Paganism.

Paul and the Corinthians
Paul visited Corinth during his second missionary journey, probably in A.D. 50. Having been in some peril in Macedonia, he fled by ship to Athens (Acts 17:5-15). Not meeting with great success there (Acts 17:16-34), he then journeyed the short distance to Corinth where he met up with Priscilla and Aquila (Acts 18:1f). At first, he preached in the synagogue with some success (including winning to Christ the ruler of the synagogue). But then the Jews became resistive and forced him to leave. So he moved next door to the synagogue, into the home of a Gentile. The Jews eventually hauled Paul before the new governor, Gallio, hoping to silence him, but Gallio threw the case out of court as having no merit. After some 18 months (his longest stay anywhere except Ephesus), Paul left and continued his missionary work in Syria.

Two events sparked the writing of 1 Corinthians some three or four years later. First, he heard that there was a divisive spirit loose in the church (1 Corinthians 1:11). Second, he received a letter in which the Corinthians asked him questions about marriage (1 Corinthians 7:1) and other matters. In addition a delegation came from Corinth that filled in his knowledge of the problem there (1 Corinthians 16:15-17). Being unable to visit them personally, he sought to deal with the issues by letter and thus the Corinthian correspondence was begun.

Theme
1 Corinthians is a practical, issue-oriented letter in which Paul tells his readers what they ought to do or not do. Paul's pattern in other letters, typically, is to begin with a strong theological statement and then follow up with insights into how these ideas apply in daily life. But not in 1 Corinthians. Here there is very little direct theological teaching. Rather Paul discusses, in turn, a number of issues of behavior.

The problem was that these proud, (sometimes) wealthy, independent ex-pagans were having a most difficult time learning how to live as Christians. It was at the level of lifestyle that paganism directed its attack on the newly emerging Christian faith. *This is the underlying issue.* Where were the lines to be drawn? How much of one's culture must be abandoned in becoming a Christian? This was a frontal attack on Christianity, which if defeated in Corinth, threatened the existence of the Christian church throughout the Empire. So just as he did in Galatians when the attack was from Judaism (over the issue of the law), Paul strikes back again here in 1 Corinthians decisively, directly without mincing words.

The Structure of 1 Corinthians

The problem in understanding 1 Corinthians is that the reader only has one side of the correspondence—Paul's. One doesn't know with certainty the questions and problems Paul is addressing. These have to be deduced. Still, it is clear that there are two major divisions in the letter. In chapters 1 through 6, Paul responds to four problems which he became aware of through the news he had received. Then in chapters 7 through 15, he responds to a series of specific questions that had been raised in a letter the Corinthians had sent him. An outline of 1 Corinthians looks like this:

I. Problems Reported to Paul (1:10—6:20)
   A. The Problem of Divisions in the Church (1:10—4:21)
   B. The Problem of Incest (5:1-13)
   C. The Problem of Lawsuits among Believers (6:1-11)
   D. The Problem of Sexual Immorality (6:12-20).

II. Questions Asked of Paul (7:1—15:58)
   A. About Marriage (7:1-24)
   B. About Virgins (7:25-40)
   C. About Food Sacrificed to Idols (8:1—11:1)
   D. About Propriety in Worship (11:2-16)
   E. About the Lord's Supper (11:17-34)
   F. About Spiritual Gifts (12:1—14:40)
   G. About the Resurrection (15:1-58)

In 1:1-9, Paul begins the letter in usual fashion while in chapter 16 he writes a concluding note.

Study Questions

1. Read the story of Paul's stay in Corinth in Acts 18. As you do so:
   (a) Keep a list of all the people he meets there.
   (b) Trace on the map the movements of people in this chapter (e.g. in verses 1 and 5).
   (c) Describe Paul's experience there.
2. Skim 1 Corinthians quickly, using the outline above, in order to get a sense of the whole book.

The World of the Early Church

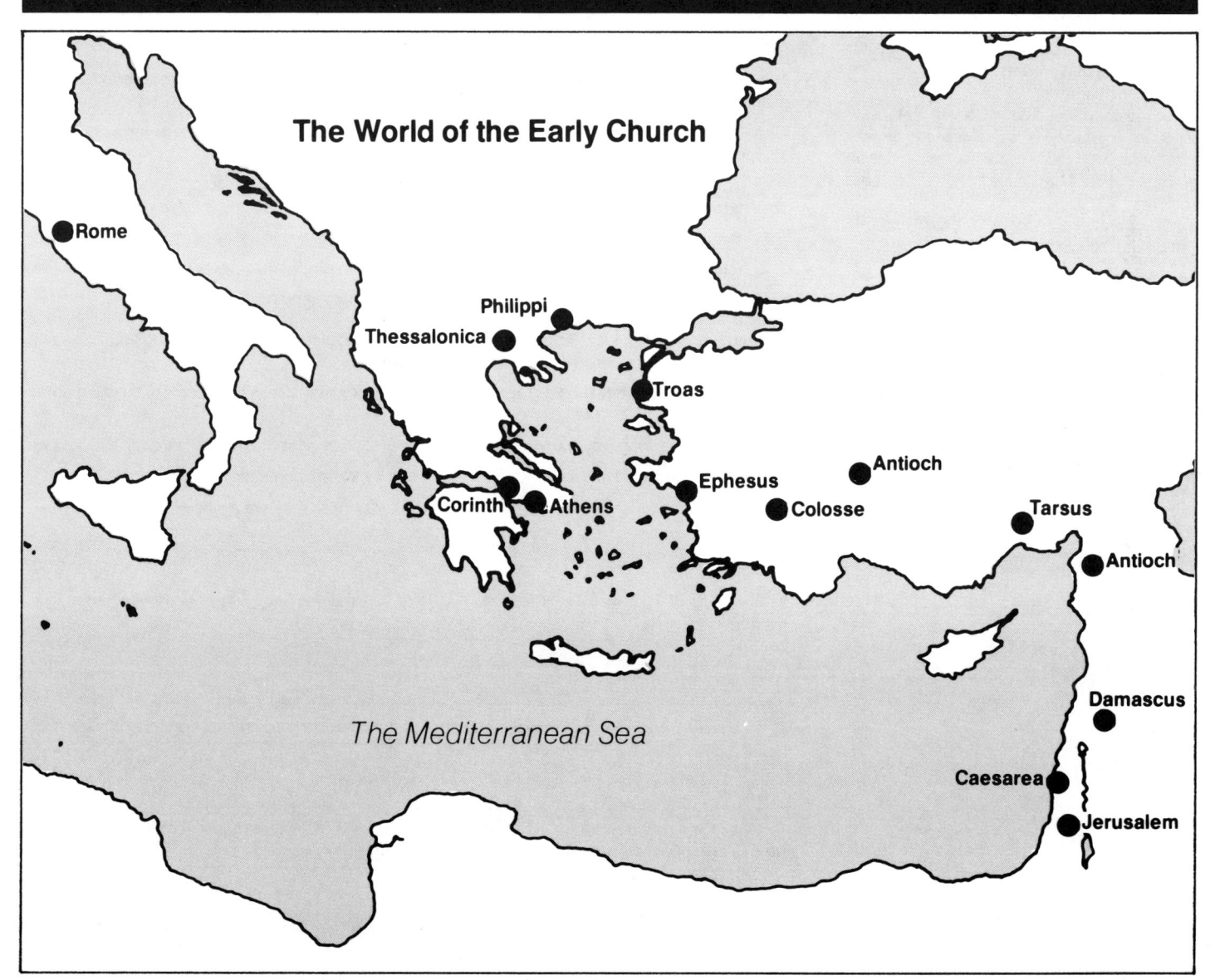

UNIT 1—Greetings and Thanksgiving/1 Corinthians 1:1-9

TEXT

1 Paul, called to be an apostle of Christ Jesus by the will of God, and our brother Sosthenes,

²To the church of God in Corinth, to those sanctified in Christ Jesus and called to be holy, together with all those everywhere who call on the name of our Lord Jesus Christ—their Lord and ours:

³Grace and peace to you from God our Father and the Lord Jesus Christ.

Thanksgiving

⁴I always thank God for you because of his grace given you in Christ Jesus. ⁵For in him you have been enriched in every way—in all your speaking and in all your knowledge—⁶because our testimony about Christ was confirmed in you. ⁷Therefore you do not lack any spiritual gift as you eagerly wait for our Lord Jesus Christ to be revealed. ⁸He will keep you strong to the end, so that you will be blameless on the day of our Lord Jesus Christ. ⁹God, who has called you into fellowship with his Son Jesus Christ our Lord, is faithful.

STUDY

READ

Two readings of the Scripture passage are suggested—each with a response to be checked or filled in on the Worksheet.

First Reading/First Impressions: To get familiar with the passage, read the passage through without stopping and record your "first impressions."

Practice: Read 1 Corinthians 1:1-9 and check the box that comes the closest to the way the passage *sounds* to you.

☐ Formal and business-like   ☐ Direct and to the point

☐ Loving and tender   ☐ Gracious and diplomatic

☐ Light and chatty   ☐ Heavy and ponderous

Second Reading/Big Idea: To get the overall idea or "gist" of the passage, as though you are seeing the action from the press box—high above the stadium.

Practice: Read 1 Corinthians 1:1-9 again and check the box that comes the closest to the main point in this passage.

☐ You've come a long way, baby   ☐ I'll be patient. God isn't through with you yet.

☐ Who said you can't have it all?   ☐ We are committed to excellence

☐ You light up my life   ☐ Praise the Lord anyhow!

SEARCH

1. From Acts 18:1-17, who was Sosthenes? What do you imagine happened to him since those events?

2. What does the way Paul defines the church (v. 2) indicate about his emphasis in this letter?

3. "Grace and peace" (v. 3) is a common greeting Paul uses. What illustrations from the gospels or your own experience might you use to explain what those terms mean?

4. In verses 4-7, Paul is thankful for several things about the church in Corinth. What are they and how could each of these items become a problem in the church?

5. Looking over the passage as a whole, what facts about Jesus does Paul mention? Why are these especially important for a church that is facing internal problems?

APPLY

As you begin this course, what are some goals you would like to work on? Check one or two from the list below and add anything specific in the box.
☐ To get to know God in a more personal way
☐ To understand what I believe as a Christian and where I stand on issues
☐ To develop my skills in Bible study and personal devotions
☐ To belong to a small group of persons who will support each other in our growth
☐ To think through my values and priorities in light of God's will
☐ To wrestle with the next step in my spiritual journey with others who care

What are you willing to commit to in the way of disciplines during the time you are in this course? Check the boxes and add anything more specific in the box.
☐ To complete the Bible study home assignment before the group meets.
☐ To attend the group meetings except in case of emergency
☐ To share in leading the group—taking my turn in rotation
☐ To keep confidential anything that is shared in the group
☐ To reach out to others who are not in a group and invite them in
☐ To attend the teaching session with the Pastor/Teacher

GROUP AGENDA

Every group meeting has three parts: (1) gathering (15 minutes) for coffee and announcements, (2) sharing (30-45 minutes) for Bible study, and (3) caring (15 minutes) for prayer requests and prayer. When you get to the SHARING/BIBLE STUDY, divide into groups of four (4 at the dining table, 4 at the kitchen table, etc.) and use the flow questions below.

TO BEGIN/10 Minutes (Choose 1 or 2)

☐ As a child, what was your favorite team of heroes? (Batman and Robin? The Lone Ranger and Tonto? Luke Skywalker and Hans Solo?) Who was your partner as a kid? ☐ Where do you like to go now when you need peace and quiet? ☐ What did you jot down for READ?

TO GO DEEPER/20 Minutes (Choose 2 or 3)

☐ If you did not go over the Introduction (p. 9) in your Orientation Session, take a few minutes to do so now. ☐ Share the results of the SEARCH part of your Bible study, one person giving an answer to number one, the next person to number two, etc. ☐ In verse 2, what does it mean to be sanctified and holy? ☐ How do you account for Paul's sense of hope as he writes to such a difficult group of people? ☐ Case History: Bob has lived a pretty wild life—drugs, sleeping around, giving his family lots of headaches. Suddenly Bob has a dramatic conversion experience and goes around pushing his new experience on his friends. How would you deal with Bob as a friend?

TO CLOSE/5-20 minutes (Choose 1 or 2)

☐ What did you put down for APPLY? ☐ Where do you need a little "grace" and "peace" in your life right now? Where have you experienced it this past year? ☐ What is one thing you would like to get out of this study?

NOTES ON 1 CORINTHIANS 1:1-9

Summary: Paul begins this letter in conventional Greek fashion. He defines the sender(s) and the recipients and then offers a greeting. Following this in vv. 4-9 he gives thanks for the Corinthians, again quite typical of how Paul began letters.

v. 1 **an apostle** ... Paul does not always identify himself by his title (e.g., I Thessalonians 1:1). He may do so here because his authority as an apostle is an issue with the Corinthians. In 2 Corinthians, especially, he will deal directly with this problem. An *apostle* is 'one who is sent,' 'an envoy.' It is an office held by those who witnessed the resurrected Christ and were called by Christ to this position. Their special job was to plant new churches throughout the Roman Empire.

by the will of God ... Paul did not just decide that he would like to be an apostle and so proclaim himself one. God made it quite clear that *He* had chosen Paul for this task (Acts 22:21). In other words, superior qualifications alone are not sufficient to entitle a person to this or any other job in the church.

our brother ... Sosthenes is not an apostle. He is, however, a son of God the Father and thus part of God's family (as are all Christians) which is the basis on which Christians are meant to relate to one another—as kin, with sharing, care, and patient love.

Sosthenes ... it is possible that this is the same Sosthenes who was the leader of the synagogue (the former leader Crispus having been converted—Acts 18:8) when the Jews brought Paul before Gallio, the proconsul, in an effort to have Paul sent to jail. The Jews took out their frustration at their failure to have Paul silenced by beating up Sosthenes outside the court (Acts 18:17). Perhaps he later became a Christian and joined Paul as a partner in ministry.

v. 2 **to the church** ... Paul sends his letter to the whole body of Christians in Corinth, expecting it to be read publicly.

sanctified ... consecrated, dedicated to the service of God.

called ... in the same way that Paul was called to be an apostle (v. 1), every believer is called by God to be holy.

holy ... to be set apart to serve God's purposes, in much the same fashion as in the Old Testament where priests were set apart to serve a special religious function. In the New Testament all believers are "saints" (i.e., holy persons). Paul has probably borrowed the phrase in verse 2 **called to be holy** from the Greek Old Testament where it is one of the terms for Israel and means "called to be God's holy people" with the emphasis both on their being *holy* and being *his* people.

together with ... not only are the Corinthian Christians called to holiness, so too are all Christians.

their Lord and ours ... the call to a common holiness springs from the fact of having a common Lord. This may be an indirect jab at their individualism—they are neither the first nor the only ones to become his people, but they are acting as if they were!

v. 3 **Grace and peace** ... here Paul alters the standard greeting. At this point in a letter a Greek would have said "greetings" (*chairein*) but Paul shifts this to "grace" (*charis*). On the other hand, a Jew would have said "peace" which Paul does include in his greeting. *Grace* is that unmerited gift of God by which a person comes into salvation and grows thereafter. *Peace* is the outcome of that salvation, and has the idea of "wholeness" and "health."

v. 4-9 ... Paul must face some very difficult issues in this letter. But rather than plunging right in with a spirit of judgment and a list of rules, he begins with thanksgiving. Whatever irregularities might exist at Corinth, they do so in the context of the good work that God has done in their midst.

v. 4 **I** ... in fact, it is Paul who is writing. Sosthenes joined him only in the general greeting.

v. 5 **in every way** ... gifts of grace include salvation itself (v. 2), special supernatural gifts (v. 5), and confidence of acquittal on the day of Judgment (v. 8).

all your speaking ... by this he probably refers to the gift of tongues (12:10); to prophecy (14:1); to messages of wisdom and knowledge (12:8), etc. In Corinth, the oratory of philosophers was common and valued. The Christians too, it seems, as part of their *riches* in Christ, had been given various speech-related abilities. This, however, has led to problems in the church with which Paul will have to deal in this letter.

knowledge . . . the ability to understand and apply Christian truth. *Knowledge* is a frequent theme in the two Corinthian letters, appearing 16 times, in comparison to Paul's use of the term only seven other times in the rest of his letters. Their knowledge, while undoubtedly real and a gift of grace, had also led to problems. Paul is grateful for the very thing that has gone astray!

v. 7 **you do not lack any spiritual gift** . . . this is said both seriously (since Christians have at their disposal all of God's grace-gifts) and tongue-in-cheek (as Paul echoes their own boasting). In fact "the troubles in Corinth were due not to a deficiency of gifts but to lack of proportion and balance in estimating and using them" (Barrett).

spiritual gifts . . . *charismata,* Paul's word for the special gifts given by God such as the gift of healing or of speaking in tongues. These gifts had a special fascination for the Corinthians. They serve as direct witnesses to the supernatural nature of Christianity. They spring from the general fact of grace (v. 4) and are specific examples of the operation of God's grace.

to be revealed . . . at the end of time, history will be concluded when Christ returns and ushers in the new kingdom. Until that moment Christians live in eager expectation, with foretastes of what one day will be normative.

v. 8 **blameless** . . . Christians need not fear judgment since Jesus himself will keep them strong, just as he has already secured their acquittal by his death.

day of our Lord Jesus Christ . . . the Day of Judgment

v. 9 **called** . . . the Christian life is ultimately a calling and depends on God's initiative.

COMMENTS

The Church at Corinth

The membership of the Corinthian church reflected the diverse and cosmopolitan nature of the city itself. There were some Jews in the congregation but it was mainly Gentile. There were some wealthy people but most were working-class people including slaves. Despite these differences they did share some things in common. They all had been influenced by the permissive, pagan atmosphere of the city. They were not necessarily great intellectuals, but they were very fond of "wisdom" and "knowledge" and came to pride themselves in their possession of it. They were all much taken with the so-called "supernatural" gifts of the Holy Spirit—like speaking in tongues, prophesying, and so forth.

This was not a group that probably would have been drawn together in the normal course of affairs except for the fact that they had met Jesus and he had changed their lives. They didn't know a lot about Jesus yet, and when it came to lifestyle, they certainly muddled Christianity and culture together in a confused and unhealthy way. But they had started down the right road together. With God's grace, Paul's instruction, and the Holy Spirit's power, they would learn and grow. It would have been an exciting church to attend, though in all honesty, it was probably far too bizarre a place for most of us to feel comfortable joining!

UNIT 2—Divisions in the Church/1 Corinthians 1:10-17

TEXT

Divisions in the Church

¹⁰I appeal to you, brothers, in the name of our Lord Jesus Christ, that all of you agree with one another so that there may be no divisions among you and that you may be perfectly united in mind and thought. ¹¹My brothers, some from Chloe's household have informed me that there are quarrels among you. ¹²What I mean is this: One of you says, "I follow Paul"; another, "I follow Apollos"; another, "I follow Cephas[a]"; still another, "I follow Christ."

¹³Is Christ divided? Was Paul crucified for you? Were you baptized into[b] the name of Paul? ¹⁴I am thankful that I did not baptize any of you except Crispus and Gaius, ¹⁵so no one can say that you were baptized into my name. ¹⁶(Yes, I also baptized the household of Stephanas; beyond that, I don't remember if I baptized anyone else.) ¹⁷For Christ did not send me to baptize, but to preach the gospel—not with words of human wisdom, lest the cross of Christ be emptied of its power.

[a]12 *That is, Peter*   [b]13 *Or* in; *also in verse 15*

STUDY

READ

First Reading/First Impressions
The closest thing in my experience to what the Corinthian church sounds like here is...
☐ attending a political convention. ☐ talking sports at work. ☐ talking religion at home. ☐ _____

Second Reading/Big Idea
As an editor for "The Corinthian Enquirer," come up with a sensational headline that catches the problem here.

SEARCH

1. What are three parts to Paul's plea? (v. 10) Hint: look for the "thats."

2. What tensions appear to be threatening the unity in this church? (vv. 11-12, 15)

3. Paul, Cephas (the apostle Peter), and Christ are well known, but from Acts 18:24-19:1 write a short biography of Apollos.

16

4. Write a sentence focusing on how each group might have boasted about their "leader." (Example: "It's best to follow Paul because, like me, God spoke to him in a vision.") See notes as well.

Paul:

Apollos:

Peter:

Christ:

5. What do these arguments reveal about how at least some of the people viewed Christ?

6. How does Paul undercut these divisions over which leader to follow? (v. 13)

APPLY

What is a special contribution that some Christian group or denomination has made to your life? Has that strength ever been a cause of your doubting the "worth" of Christians coming from other traditions that do not display that strength so much? How?

Who are the significant people in your own spiritual development? Fill in the coaching staff below with the people who have played a part in your life.

RECRUITER: (reached out to me for Christ) _____

HEAD COACH: (taught me the fundamentals) _____

ASSISTANT COACH: (provided back-up/support) _____

TRAINER: (handy with aches, pains, injuries) _____

HEAD CHEERLEADER: (my biggest fan) _____

GROUP AGENDA

Remember, every meeting has three parts: (1) Gathering (15 minutes) for coffee and announcements, (2) Sharing (30-45 minutes) for Bible study, and (3) Caring (15 minutes) for prayer requests and prayer. When you get to the SHARING/BIBLE STUDY, divide into groups of four (4 at the dining table, 4 at the kitchen table, etc.) and use the flow questions below.

TO BEGIN/10 Minutes (Choose 1 or 2)

☐ When you were growing up, what was the major cause for quarrels between you and your brother or sister? Between you and your parents? ☐ Who (a real live person) did you follow and almost idolize when you were a child? Who did you look up to as a teenager? ☐ Who was one of the best communicators you've ever heard—radio, TV, on tape, in person? What was it about this person that made them this way? ☐ What did you jot down under READ in the Bible Study?

TO GO DEEPER/20 Minutes (Choose 2 or 3)

☐ Share what you jotted down under SEARCH in your Bible study, one person sharing question one, the next person question two, etc. ☐ What light does this passage shed on the cause of "divisions" in the church today? What can be done about this? ☐ What are some of the issues that divide the church today? ☐ Case History: Your close friend Mary has "fallen in love" with a certain radio preacher. "Nobody preaches the gospel like So and So," she says. What do you advise?

TO CLOSE/5-20 Minutes (Choose 1 or 2)

☐ What did you put down for APPLY? ☐ Who was one of your spiritual heroes or mentors? What from his or her life do you want to build into your own?

NOTES ON 1 CORINTHIANS 1:10-17

Section Summary/1 Corinthians 1:10—4:21: The first problem that Paul deals with is divisions in the church. Ever since Apollos and (probably) Peter visited the church, people began to pick sides, some preferring one leader, some another. Some even became opponents of Paul. It seems that the Corinthians had begun to view Christianity as a new philosophy ("wisdom") and the apostles were regarded (and judged) as if they were itinerant philosophers. Paul attacks the problem on two levels. After defining the problem (1:10-12), he first launches into an explanation of divine wisdom (1:13—2:16). The gospel is not merely another philosophy, he says. Then second, after a transition paragraph (3:1-4), he corrects their views of Christian teachers (3:5—4:21). They are not mere philosophers who are competing with one another. They are all servants of the same God and it is wrong to pit one leader against another.

v. 10 **I appeal to you** ... I beg you, I beseech you.... This matter of their divisions is serious and must be dealt with.

brothers ... This is the basis of his appeal. Paul can write this way because they are all related to one another. It is not merely a matter of belonging to the same organization. They are part of the same family.

agree with one another ... "make up your differences," "let go of your party slogans" ... This is the first of three "that" clauses in verse 10 describing what Paul desires for the Corinthian Christians.

divisions ... **schismata** (from which the English word *schisms* comes); a word often used to describe tears in a piece of clothing.

perfectly united ... This Greek word is used to describe the knitting back together of broken bones or the mending of fishing nets (Mark 1:19).

mind and thought ... This disunity is rooted in differing ideas (doctrines). To be restored ("perfectly united"), i.e., to knit back together the church which is torn apart, requires a unity of understanding.

v. 11 **Chloe's household** ... Paul is writing from Ephesus. The slaves (or freedmen) of an Ephesian woman named Chloe had visited the church in Corinth and brought back the story of the disunity there.

quarrels ... it seems that total dissension had not yet occurred amongst the Corinthians but strong arguments were taking place.

v. 12 ... These are the slogans of the contending parties. Various Christian leaders unwittingly have become rallying points for dissension. It is important to notice these slogans because they are the first of a series of slogans to which Paul must respond (e.g., see 6:12 and 7:1).

I follow Paul ... Paul does not commend those "on his side." A faction in his name is no better than any other faction. In fact, these folks had probably exaggerated and falsified his actual viewpoints. (This was probably the Gentile party.)

I follow Apollos ... After he had been instructed in the gospel by Priscilla and Aquila, Apollos went to Corinth to assist the church there. A bright, articulate Jew from Alexandria with great skill in debate (Acts 18:24—19) would seem to be a natural leader for those who attempted to intellectualize Christianity. "It is easy to understand that, in a church where gifts of the tongue were rated high (1:5; 12:8; 14:26), the appearance of a particularly eloquent preacher should awaken partisanship, and some contempt for the founder, who was despised as a speaker (2 Corinthians 10:10) and himself acknowledged his failings in this regard (2 Corinthians 11:6)" (Barrett).

I follow Cephas ... It is probable that Peter also visited Corinth. This faction probably would have been oriented towards a more Jewish Christianity.

I follow Christ ... These are possibly the people who look with some disdain on the other groups who profess allegiance to the Christ preached by Paul or by Apollos or by Cephas. Instead they profess allegiance to the Christ they know without the teaching of anyone. This may even be a mystical or gnostic-like party given to inner visions and revelations.

1:13—2:5 ... by their strife and their factions they misrepresent (and misunderstand) the gospel. It is not, at its root, merely the most articulate available explanation of what is true in the universe. The gospel was not derived from human speculation. In fact, it was totally unexpected. It has to do with weakness and death and, on human terms, seemed quite foolish.

v. 13 ... Paul makes his point by means of three rhetorical questions. The answer to each question is clearly "No."

COMMENTS

v. 14 **baptize** ... Paul is not belittling this rite of incorporation into the church. He did indeed baptize some people (vv. 15-16). But his ministry was elsewhere (v. 17). He was primarily a gospel preacher. In any case, his point is that it does not matter *who* baptized a person. Baptism is *into the name of Christ* and all baptized people belong to Christ alone, utterly and completely, since baptism into a name signifies ownership by that person.

Crispus ... Acts 18:8.

Gaius ... probably Paul's host in Corinth when he wrote the Epistle to the Romans (Romans 16:23).

v. 16 **Stephanas** ... See 16:17.

v. 17 Here Paul comes to the principle that lies at the root of the problem in Corinth. They can form such factions only because they misunderstand the nature of God's wisdom.

preach the gospel ... Paul's call was to evangelism. He gave himself to preaching the gospel and left to others the work of incorporating believers into the church. He is careful to indicate here that this was preaching, not rhetoric (*"not with words of human wisdom"*).

wisdom ... *sophia,* a key word in 1 Corinthians. Paul uses the words *wisdom* and *wise* a total of 45 times in his letters. Twenty-six of these occurrences are here in 1 Corinthians 1-3. Although Paul uses the word in both positive and negative ways, here the idea is negative. This is *wisdom* defined as the skillful use of human reason with a view to convincing the hearer of the truth of a position.

lest the cross of Christ be emptied ... that is, lest it "dwindle to nothing, vanish under the weight of rhetorical argument and dialectic subtlety" (Lightfoot). Paul is eager that people be persuaded by Christ crucified and not by mere eloquence.

Cephas and Corinth

Did Cephas (Peter) actually visit Corinth? Is this why there is a party there in his name? Paul taught in Corinth. Apollos taught there. Cannot a strong case be made that Peter must have taught there?

In fact, scholars are divided on this issue. Still there is interesting evidence that points to the possibility that Peter might well have come to Corinth. For one thing, we know Paul won converts in Corinth as had Apollos. It is not unreasonable to suppose Peter had done so also and these are the folk who are members of his (unauthorized) party.

Then there is the evidence that Peter did travel outside Jerusalem. From Galatians 2:11 we know he was in Antioch. It must also be noted that he writes to Christians in Pontus, Galatia, Cappadocia, Asia and Bithynia in his letter (1 Peter 1:1) and this would lend support to his having worked in the northeastern Mediterranean region. And of course, Corinth is just a boat trip across the Aegean Sea from that region. Other Christian literature from the post-apostolic era (the Clementine literature) ascribes widespread missionary activity to Peter (Dionysius also wrote that both Peter and Paul "planted and taught" the Corinthian church, but he deduced this from 1 Corinthians!). It does, therefore, seem quite possible that members of the church in Corinth knew Peter directly rather than just deciding to rally around the banner of this prominent apostle about whom they had heard.

Yet other scholars have suggested that indeed the core of the Cephas party consisted of people converted and baptized by Peter, but that this had happened elsewhere and they had later migrated to Corinth. Once there, they were scandalized by what was going on and so formed themselves into a party within the church for the purpose of bringing it more in line with their prior experience of Christianity in their original churches. This would probably have been a Jewish form of Christianity.

UNIT 3—Christ the Wisdom and Power of God / 1 Cor. 1:18-2:5

TEXT

Christ the Wisdom and Power of God

18For the message of the cross is foolishness to those who are perishing, but to us who are being saved it is the power of God. 19For it is written:

"I will destroy the wisdom of the wise; the intelligence of the intelligent I will frustrate."[a]

20Where is the wise man? Where is the scholar? Where is the philosopher of this age? Has not God made foolish the wisdom of the world? 21For since in the wisdom of God the world through its wisdom did not know him, God was pleased through the foolishness of what was preached to save those who believe. 22Jews demand miraculous signs and Greeks look for wisdom, 23but we preach Christ crucified: a stumbling block to Jews and foolishness to Gentiles, 24but to those whom God has called, both Jews and Greeks, Christ the power of God and the wisdom of God. 25For the foolishness of God is wiser than man's wisdom, and the weakness of God is stronger than man's strength.

26Brothers, think of what you were when you were called. Not many of you were wise by human standards; not many were influential; not many were of noble birth. 27But God chose the foolish things of the world to shame the wise; God chose the weak things of the world to shame the strong. 28He chose the lowly things of this world and the despised things—and the things that are not—to nullify the things that are, 29so that no one may boast before him. 30It is because of him that you are in Christ Jesus, who has become for us wisdom from God—that is, our righteousness, holiness and redemption. 31Therefore, as it is written: "Let him who boasts boast in the Lord."[b]

2 When I came to you, brothers, I did not come with eloquence or superior wisdom as I proclaimed to you the testimony about

Continued on next page

STUDY

READ

First Reading/First Impressions

What's going on here? ☐ Paul is being anti-intellectual. ☐ Paul is pointing out the limits of human knowledge. ☐ Paul is pointing out God's power as opposed to human power. ☐ _____

Second Reading/Big Idea

Put what you see as the main verse here in your own words.

SEARCH

1. What can you learn from the following verses about the type of "wisdom and strength" that held such an attraction for the Corinthians?

(1:20-21)

(1:26)

(2:1)

(2:4-5)

2. In contrast, what do you learn about the "wisdom and power" of God?

(1:18)

(1:21)

(1:24-25)

(1:27-29)

(1:30)

(2:4-5)

3. Do you think Paul is rejecting education itself, or the prideful assumption that spiritual knowledge is a product of superior human intellect? Why? In light of this church's divisions, what is his point? (v. 31)

4. How would you define what Paul means by the four terms he uses to describe what Christ is for those who trust him? (1:30)

wisdom (see also Col. 2:2, 8-10)

righteousness (see also Rom. 3:22)

holiness (see also Gal. 2:20)

redemption (see also 1 Pet. 1:18-19)

APPLY

On the chart below indicate where you are at the moment in your own understanding of the Christian message. Then go back and fill in significant dates, places or events when you moved from one development stage to another.

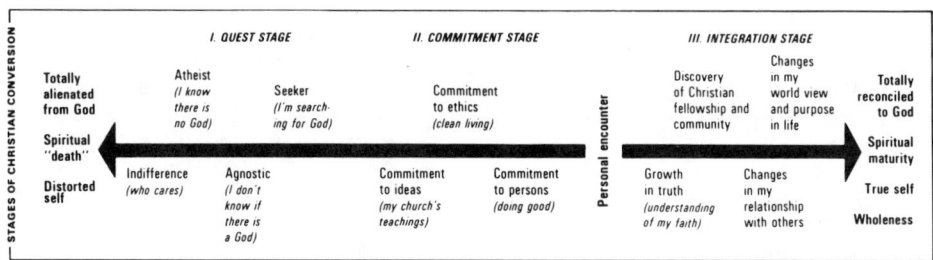

STAGES OF CHRISTIAN CONVERSION	I. QUEST STAGE		II. COMMITMENT STAGE			III. INTEGRATION STAGE		
Totally alienated from God	Atheist (I know there is no God)	Seeker (I'm searching for God)	Commitment to ethics (clean living)			Discovery of Christian fellowship and community	Changes in my world view and purpose in life	Totally reconciled to God
Spiritual "death"					Personal encounter			Spiritual maturity
Distorted self	Indifference (who cares)	Agnostic (I don't know if there is a God)	Commitment to ideas (my church's teachings)	Commitment to persons (doing good)		Growth in truth (understanding of my faith)	Changes in my relationship with others	True self
								Wholeness

*The idea for this chart is taken from Dick Peace's book "Pilgrimage" by Acton House.

GROUP AGENDA

Divide into groups of 4 before you start to share and follow the time recommendations.

TO BEGIN/10 Minutes (Choose 1 or 2)

☐ When you were a child, who did you think was one of the wisest people in the world? When you were a teenager? A young adult? ☐ If you could have good looks, great strength, or a superb mind, what would you choose? Why? ☐ Were the people who contributed the most to your spiritual life more gifted in knowledge, encouragement or love? ☐ What did you jot down under READ?

TO GO DEEPER/20 Minutes (Choose 2 or 3)

☐ Share the SEARCH portion of the Bible study, one question at a time. One person share an answer to question one, the next person question two, etc. ☐ Go back and read Isaiah 29:14. How does Paul use this passage? ☐ Why is it that intelligent, proud people so often miss the point of the cross? ☐ In contemporary society what are the philosophers and brilliant thinkers looking to for salvation? ☐ Case History: Your close friend gave up his personal faith in college. "There may be a God somewhere," he says, "but I can't live my life on blind assumptions." What do you say?

Continued on next page

God.[c] ²For I resolved to know nothing while I was with you except Jesus Christ and him crucified. ³I came to you in weakness and fear, and with much trembling. ⁴My message and my preaching were not with wise and persuasive words, but with a demonstration of the Spirit's power, ⁵so that your faith might not rest on men's wisdom, but on God's power.

[a]19 Isaiah 29:14   [b]31 Jer. 9:24   [c]1 Some manuscripts *as I proclaimed to you God's mystery*

NOTES ON 1 CORINTHIANS 1:18-2:5

Summary: The fact that the Corinthians can boast of party slogans is a clear indication that they overvalue human wisdom and misunderstand the nature of the gospel. In the light of this Paul explains in verses 18-25 the difference between human and divine wisdom. He shows that the gospel is decidedly not a species of human philosophy—because it involves such a reversal of human expectation. Who would have thought that God would work through the scandal of the cross? Only God could demonstrate his power through a dying, powerless, "criminal." Paul then goes on to "prove" that God does indeed work through weakness. He first looks at the Corinthians (verses 26-31) and then at himself (2:1-5), pointing out that they were not very clever and he was not very persuasive, so the fact they are Christians "proves" that God works through weakness. How else could the fact of the church at Corinth be explained?

v. 18 **the message of the cross** ... This is the only legitimate slogan. Paul immediately puts the issue in stark terms: the question of eternal destiny hinges upon the meaning of the cross. Their misunderstanding and the resultant division is no slight matter. It strikes at the core of the gospel.

foolishness ... It is absurd to many that at the center of God's redemptive activity lies death by crucifixion. Note that the opposite of *foolishness* is not *wisdom,* but (God's) *power.*

Those who are perishing ... Paul's way of describing those who are on their way to exclusion from God's kingdom. Unless they repent (turn around and go the other way), they will not be acquitted on the Day of Judgment.

being saved ... Salvation is a process, begun at conversion, consummated at the Second Coming, and fulfilled in the New Age.

v. 19 ... Paul quotes the Old Testament to demonstrate that indeed human-centered wisdom will be overthrown by God.

v. 20 ... All those who represent human wisdom are forced to flee in the face of God's revelation that their wisdom is actually mere folly.

v. 21 ... The wisdom of God "is not a plan that men would ever have thought of because it operates through Christian preaching which, since it is focused upon the cross (v. 18) will inevitably be judged by worldly standards to be not wisdom but folly" (Barrett).

v. 22 **Jews demand miraculous signs** ... The Jews expected a Messiah who would come in obvious power doing miraculous deeds. In Jesus they saw one so weak that his enemies got away with killing him. "To the Jew, a crucified Messiah was an impossible contradiction, like 'cooked ice' " (Fee). The Jews demanded that God certify his activity by means of supernatural acts.

Greeks look for wisdom ... Their delight was in clever, cunning logic delivered with soaring persuasiveness. The idea that a Jewish peasant who died as a convicted criminal could be the focus of God's redemptive plan for the world was so silly as to be laughable.

v. 23 ... To accept the word of the cross is to accept that we as people are weak, sinful, and helpless before God. It is to accept that we cannot understand God on our own nor devise ways to reach him by ourselves. We must trust God, not our human wisdom and power, and this is a scandal to many.

stumbling block ... Literally, "a scandal." Jesus' crucifixion "proved" that he could not be of God since according to Deuteronomy 21:23, those hanging from a tree are cursed of God. A suffering, dying Messiah was totally outside first-century Jewish expectations.

foolishness ... Both the incarnation and the crucifixion are totally unexpected. The Greeks felt that gods would not act like that. In fact, the cradle and the cross show that people cannot reach God via the route of wisdom and reason but only by the response of faith to that which has been done for them.

v. 24 ... In fact, Christ is indeed both the sign that is craved by the Jews (he is the power

---

GROUP AGENDA continued

TO CLOSE/5-20 Minutes (Choose 1 or 2)

☐ Where did you find yourself on the Spiritual Understanding chart? ☐ How did you feel about the message of Christianity *before* you became a Christian? ☐ What are some contemporary pictures that come to mind when you think about powerful, successful people? How do those ideas sometimes conflict with your following Christ? ☐ When you present the Gospel to someone, how do you do it? ☐ In what way do you find God is still using the foolish, the weak, the lowly, the despised to accomplish his purpose?

of God) and the ultimate truth desired by the Greeks (he is the wisdom of God).

v. 25 ... There is indeed a paradox at the heart of the gospel, at least when the gospel is viewed through the lens of human wisdom. But in actual fact Christ crucified conveys the truth about God and provides the power to break human bondage.

v. 26 think of what you were ... In fact, in their own calling one sees this same paradox: the all-powerful God using the "weak things of the world."

not many ... The early church had special appeal to the poor and to those with little social standing. This was part of its offensiveness to the culture in general. The "wrong" people were attracted to it. On the other hand, it is clear that there were some influential people in the Corinthian Church. For example, there was Crispus, a former head of the synagogue who had a position of status in the Jewish community (Acts 18:8), and there was Erastus, who as director of public works in Corinth, was a man of wealth and power (Romans 16:23).

v. 27 The foolish things of the world ... Those who in the *estimation of the current culture* were insignificant.

to shame ... By proving that the wise men were, in fact, quite wrong.

v. 28 lowly ... The opposite of "noble birth" in verse 26.

v. 29 ... A church composed of such folk ought to have a better grasp of what the gospel is all about because they would know that it was not on account of who they were or what they had done, that they were chosen. There ought to be, therefore, no false boasting within the church. To *boast* is to wrongly evaluate one's own gifts, put confidence in them, and to express this with a tinge of pride. Such boasting was one of the problems in the Corinthian church.

v. 30 because of him ... They owe the fact that they are related to God solely to Jesus Christ.

wisdom from God ... Paul spoke of "human wisdom" in verse 17, i.e., philosophical wisdom. But here he begins to "de-philosophize" *sophia* (wisdom) and instead historicize it. The historical Jesus, not some philosophical proposition, is God's wisdom. It is Christ who mediates God's plan of salvation. *Righteousness, holiness,* and *redemption* are three of Paul's metaphors for salvation.

righteousness ... Christ is *our righteousness* in that he took upon himself the guilt of human sin. So on the Last Day when Christians stand before the Judge, they are viewed not in terms of their own failure and inadequacy but as being "in Christ." Thus his righteousness assures them of acquittal.

holiness ... Human beings cannot come before a Holy God because they are not holy; but once again Christ provides what people lack. His holiness suffices for them and so a relationship with God is assured.

redemption ... It is by Christ's redeeming work on the cross that wisdom, righteousness and holiness are mediated to humankind.

2:1-5 ... Paul shows that, in fact, his own ministry amongst them was a demonstration of the principles outlined in 1:18-31.

v. 1 eloquence or superior wisdom ... "The two nouns are close together in meaning, for *eloquence* (literally, *logos* or 'word') here is rational talk, and *wisdom* worldly cleverness. They represent the outward and inward means by which men may commend a case, effectiveness of language, and skill of argumentation" (Barrett).

v. 2 ... In Corinth, a city teeming with articulate philosophers, Paul's refusal to make persuasive speech and brilliant logic preeminent in his evangelism was especially striking. Instead he simply preached (not "orated") the crucified Christ (a paradox to most).

v. 3 ... Not for his own safety but because of the awesome responsibility he had as a preacher of the gospel.

v. 4 ... Paul says he was not an impressive speaker (2 Corinthians 10:1), even though his writing (which was spoken to a scribe and has the "feel" of speech) is often quite eloquent. As E. Norden wrote: "In these passages (Romans 8 and 1 Corinthians 13) the diction of the Apostle rises to the height of Plato's in the *Phaedrus*."

demonstration of the Spirit's power ... Paul here reveals the secret behind the impact that his preaching made. People were moved, not by his human eloquence, but by the inner, convicting power of the Holy Spirit. This is the real proof of the validity of the gospel.

UNIT 4—Wisdom From the Spirit / 1 Corinthians 2:6-16

TEXT

Wisdom from the Spirit

⁶We do, however, speak a message of wisdom among the mature, but not the wisdom of this age or of the rulers of this age, who are coming to nothing. ⁷No, we speak of God's secret wisdom, a wisdom that has been hidden and that God destined for our glory before time began. ⁸None of the rulers of this age understood it, for if they had, they would not have crucified the Lord of glory. ⁹However, as it is written:

"No eye has seen,
   no ear has heard,
no mind has conceived
   what God has prepared for those who love him"[a] —

¹⁰but God has revealed it to us by his Spirit.

The Spirit searches all things, even the deep things of God. ¹¹For who among men knows the thoughts of a man except the man's spirit within him? In the same way no one knows the thoughts of God except the Spirit of God. ¹²We have not received the spirit of the world but the Spirit who is from God, that we may understand what God has freely given us. ¹³This is what we speak, not in words taught us by human wisdom but in words taught by the Spirit, expressing spiritual truths in spiritual words.[b] ¹⁴The man without the Spirit does not accept the things that come from the Spirit of God, for they are foolishness to him, and he cannot understand them, because they are spiritually discerned. ¹⁵The spiritual man makes judgments about all things, but he himself is not subject to any man's judgment:

¹⁶"For who has known the mind of the Lord
   that he may instruct him?"[c]

But we have the mind of Christ.

[a] 9 Isaiah 64:4 [b] 13 Or *Spirit, interpreting spiritual truths to spiritual men* [c] 16 Isaiah 40:13

STUDY

READ

First Reading/First Impressions
How do you feel about Paul's message here? ☐ It's crystal clear what he means. ☐ It's too spooky for me. ☐ It sounds arrogant. ☐ It's over my head. ☐ _____

Second Reading/Big Idea
How would you condense this passage into one or two sentences?

SEARCH

1. Look at all the references to "wisdom" in this passage. Jot down the reference and any information about the subject in that verse. Then, using this information as well as the insight gained from SEARCH questions 1 and 2 in the last chapter, write out a short summary of what you learn about the differences between human wisdom and God's wisdom.

2. What point is Paul making by his quote from the Old Testament in verse 9? (see also v. 7)

3. Philosophers were respected as people who could search out deep truths. In contrast, what is Paul saying about how the truth of the gospel is discovered? (vv. 10-13) Why is that significant for their unity?

4. From verse 9, how does the condition for receiving this spiritual wisdom differ from the conditions necessary to gain the world's wisdom? Why is that significant for their unity?

5. How might verses 15-16 help those who were feeling put down by others as not being "spiritual enough" or for following the "wrong" leader? (see 1:12)

APPLY

The Corinthians were measuring "truth" by how powerful, influential, and articulate someone was. Think of some expressions of this idea today. Pick one that affects the way you decide whether or not someone (like yourself!) is "successful" or knows the truth about life. How does it square with the gospel?

(Example: The model woman is one who can have a thriving career that rivals any man's, drive a Porsche, be incredibly sexy, physically fit, etc. The pressure of that ideal on me is tremendous, but Christ says my worth is found in giving away my life for others.)

GROUP AGENDA

Divide into groups of 4 before you start to share and follow the time recommendations.

TO BEGIN/10 Minutes (Choose 1 or 2)

☐ What is one thing you remember your parents telling you that you couldn't understand "because you're too little"? How did you feel then? ☐ How well did you keep secrets when you were a child? ☐ Any good stories about when you accidentally "let the cat out of the bag"? ☐ What did you jot down under READ?

TO GO DEEPER/20 Minutes (Choose 2 or 3)

☐ Share the SEARCH portion of the Bible study, one question at a time. ☐ What do you think was going on in the church in Corinth to require this response from Paul? ☐ Read Romans 1:20. What is it about God that can be clearly understood and what requires his own Spirit to understand? ☐ How would you summarize the nature of God's wisdom in this passage? ☐ Case History: Your friend has gotten into "meditation" through her interest in karate. Her teacher is into Tai Quandu, an Oriental religion that seeks to bring the mind and the body together through meditation. As a Christian, what do you say to your friend?

TO CLOSE/5-20 Minutes (Choose 1 or 2)

☐ What did you write for APPLY? ☐ When in your spiritual journey did the "mind of Christ" start to make a difference in your values, choices and decisions? ☐ What is a particular instance in which your outlook on life has changed since becoming a Christian? ☐ In practical terms, what does it mean to you to have the "mind of Christ"? What evidence can you point to this past year in which the "mind of Christ" has given you spiritual understanding?

NOTES ON 1 CORINTHIANS 2:6-16

Summary: Paul will now qualify what he just said about his rejection of human wisdom (vv. 4-5). There is, in fact, a legitimate "message of wisdom," but, as he shows in verses 6-16 it comes from God and is discerned only by those who have the Spirit.

v. 6 **a message of wisdom** . . . Paul will now use *sophia* (wisdom) in a positive way to describe God's plan of salvation. This use of *sophia* stands in sharp contrast to that in 1:17 (see note) where wisdom is seen as persuasive human eloquence and to the uses in 1:18-25 where wisdom is evil because it makes human aspiration the criterion for truth.

among . . . Paul did not speak as some sort of elevated leader with insight no one else had. Rather the "message of wisdom" was shared in the context of the insights of other mature Christians who also had something to add (12:8).

mature . . . To be mature is to be a full-grown adult in the faith, a potential which all Christians have (Colossians 1:28) though not all experience (3:1).

but not . . . Paul first describes what God's wisdom is *not:* it is not derived from either the self-serving philosophy of fallen men and women nor from the presuppositions of the rulers.

wisdom of this age . . . In biblical thought there are two ages; "this age" in which sin and evil exist and "the age to come" when God's kingdom will be present and visible. Wisdom of this age is person-centered, and corrupted by rebellion against God—despite how it may appear on the surface.

rulers of this age . . . Sometimes this term is used to describe evil supernatural powers thought to control human destiny, but here it seems that Paul is referring to human leaders, since in verse 8 he says that these are the ones who crucified Jesus, and since the contrast in this whole passage is between the Christian (who has the Spirit), and the non-Christian (who does not).

v. 7 **God's secret wisdom** . . . In contrast to the "wisdom of the world" in which the attempt is made to show by persuasive words of rhetoric how "obvious" and "reasonable" it is, no one could have guessed God's plan. Even when it was revealed, many shunned it as "foolish" and/or scandalous (1:23).

secret . . . This is not a secret (literally *mystery*) in the sense of something that is cryptic and beyond human understanding. Rather, it means something God alone knew (it was once hidden) but which he has now revealed.

hidden . . . In the sense that God's plan of salvation was only just recently disclosed (Paul is writing some 20-30 years after the crucifixion) via the death and resurrection of Jesus, prior to which God's full intentions were known by no one.

destined for our glory . . . God always intended that humanity be redeemed and become a part of his glorious kingdom.

v. 8 **understood** . . . No one understood that Christ crucified was to be God's agent of redemption.

v. 9 . . . Paul quotes Isaiah 64:4 loosely, probably from memory.

v. 10 **revealed to us** . . . That which was hidden from the non-Christian rulers (v. 8) has now been made clear to the Christian.

by his Spirit . . . The insight referred to in verses 6-9 came not as a result of reasoning but as a result of revelation.

The Spirit searches all things . . . In Corinth, the idea was that you could by means of philosophy search out the nature of God. Paul indicates that only the Spirit himself knows and communicates accurate knowledge about God.

v. 11 . . . Paul uses an analogy to explain his point.

v. 12 **the spirit of the world** . . . An equivalent phrase to "the wisdom of this age" (v. 6).

understand . . . It is not education or intellect or occupation that yields spiritual insight. There is only one source: the Holy Spirit dwelling within a believer.

has freely given us . . . These gifts of God (v. 9) are not merely for the future but are the present experience of Christians.

v. 13 . . . The Spirit provides both understanding ("inward apprehension of profound divine truths"—v.12) and the very "language that makes conversation about these truths possible" (Barrett).

we . . . Not just Paul and his co-workers but probably all mature Christians (v. 6) have this experience—or at least the potential for it.

COMMENTS

v. 14 **the man without the Spirit** . . . In contrast to the spirit-filled person in verse 12 is the person who lacks the Holy Spirit and therefore is blind to the spiritual side of life.

v. 15 **judgments** . . . Not only does the Holy Spirit give understanding but he provides a moral standard by which to evaluate all things.

not subject to any man's judgment . . . Barrett suggests that what Paul means here is similar to what he says in 4:3-5: "human condemnation or acquittal are nothing to him. His only judge is the Lord."

v. 16 **mind of Christ** . . . Paul now shifts to this concept which parallels the idea of having the spirit of Christ.

"The Buried Life"

But often, in the world's most crowded streets,
But often, in the din of strife,
There rises an unspeakable desire
After the knowledge of our buried life:
A thirst to spend our fire and restless force
In tracking out our true, original course;
A longing to inquire
Into the mystery of this heart which beats
So wild, so deep in us—to know
Whence our lives come and where they go.

Matthew Arnold

The Chasm

by Francis A. Schaeffer

The present chasm between the generations has been brought about almost entirely by a change in the concept of truth.

Wherever you look today the new concept holds the field. The consensus about us is almost monolithic, whether you review the arts, literature or just simply read the newspapers and magazines such as *Time, Life, Newsweek, The Listener* or *The Observer*. On every side you can feel the stranglehold of this new methodology—and by "methodology" we mean the way we approach truth and knowing. It is like suffocating in a particularly bad London fog. And just as fog cannot be kept out by walls or doors, so this consensus comes in around us, till the room we live in is no longer distinct, and yet we hardly realize what has happened.

The tragedy of our situation today is that men and women are being fundamentally affected by the new way of looking at truth and yet they have never even analyzed the drift which has taken place. Young people from Christian homes are brought up in the old framework of truth. Then they are subjected to the modern framework. In time they become confused because they do not understand the alternatives with which they are being presented. Confusion becomes bewilderment, and before long they are overwhelmed. This is unhappily true not only of young people, but of many pastors, Christian educators, evangelists and missionaries as well.

So this change in the concept of the way we come to knowledge and truth is the most crucial problem, as I understand it, facing Christianity today.—Taken from *The God Who Is There* by Francis A. Schaeffer (InterVarsity Press), p. 13.

UNIT 5—On Divisions in the Church/1 Corinthians 3:1-23

TEXT

On Divisions in the Church

3 Brothers, I could not address you as spiritual but as worldly—mere infants in Christ. ²I gave you milk, not solid food, for you were not yet ready for it. Indeed, you are still not ready. ³You are still worldly. For since there is jealousy and quarreling among you, are you not worldly? Are you not acting like mere men? ⁴For when one says, "I follow Paul," and another, "I follow Apollos," are you not mere men?

⁵What, after all, is Apollos? And what is Paul? Only servants, through whom you came to believe—as the Lord has assigned to each his task. ⁶I planted the seed, Apollos watered it, but God made it grow. ⁷So neither he who plants nor he who waters is anything, but only God, who makes things grow. ⁸The man who plants and the man who waters have one purpose, and each will be rewarded according to his own labor. ⁹For we are God's fellow workers; you are God's field, God's building.

¹⁰By the grace God has given me, I laid a foundation as an expert builder, and someone else is building on it. But each one should be careful how he builds. ¹¹For no one can lay any foundation other than the one already laid, which is Jesus Christ. ¹²If any man builds on this foundation using gold, silver, costly stones, wood, hay or straw, ¹³his work will be shown for what it is, because the Day will bring it to light. It will be revealed with fire, and the fire will test the quality of each man's work. ¹⁴If what he has built survives, he will receive his reward. ¹⁵If it is burned up, he will suffer loss; he himself will be saved, but only as one escaping through the flames.

¹⁶Don't you know that you yourselves are God's temple and that God's Spirit lives in you? ¹⁷If anyone destroys God's temple, God will destroy him; for God's temple is sacred, and you are that temple.

Continued on next page

STUDY

READ

First Reading/First Impressions
It seems here that Paul is . . . ☐ scolding the Corinthians. ☐ just repeating what he's already said. ☐ trying to get the church back to the basics.

Second Reading/Big Idea
Which verse seems to be central to Paul's point here? Why?

SEARCH

1. Since each faction at Corinth thought it was more spiritual than others, how might they feel reading verses 1-3?

2. What are some of the characteristics of "worldly" versus "spiritual" people?

worldly	spiritual

3. How does the fact that the Corinthians chose sides regarding Paul and Apollos show they misunderstood the work of both?

4. What points does Paul make by use of his metaphor in verses 5-9?

5. In the metaphor of verses 9-15, what does he mean by:

Jesus as the foundation?

the different types of "building material"?

the testing of each person's work?

6. The "you" in verses 16-17 is plural, referring to the community as a whole. How would you explain to someone what Paul means by this picture (v. 16) and this warning (v. 17)?

7. How does Paul show the foolishness of their fighting over which leader to follow? (vv. 21-23; also see notes)

APPLY

If Paul wrote this letter to your community, what names might he use in place of his own and Apollos'?

What is the difference between respecting a Christian leader, and the problem Paul deals with here?

Given the clues about what makes for good "building materials," what is one "concrete" way you could contribute to the building of God's temple in your community?

GROUP AGENDA

Divide into groups of 4 before you start to share. And follow the time recommendations.

TO BEGIN/10 MINUTES (Choose 1 or 2)

☐ When you were a child, what did you build that you were proud of? ☐ How would you describe yourself in terms of a building? (tall skyscraper, little grass shack, bomb shelter, etc.) Why? ☐ What did you put down for READ?

TO GO DEEPER/20 MINUTES (Choose 2 or 3)

☐ Go around and share your answers to the SEARCH portion of the Bible study—one person taking the first question, the next person the second question, etc. ☐ What does it mean to you to "be worldly"? How can a person be a Christian and worldly at the same time? ☐ In verses 6-9, who plants? Who waters? Who is the field? Who owns the field? What does this mean in terms of the problem in the Corinthian church? ☐ Case History: Mike, who belongs to an informal house group, regularly lets you know of his disapproval of

Continued on next page

---

[18]Do not deceive yourselves. If any one of you thinks he is wise by the standards of this age, he should become a "fool" so that he may become wise. [19]For the wisdom of this world is foolishness in God's sight. As it is written: "He catches the wise in their craftiness"[a] , [20]and again, "The Lord knows that the thoughts of the wise are futile."[b] [21]So then, no more boasting about men! All things are yours, [22]whether Paul or Apollos or Cephas[c] or the world or life or death or the present or the future—all are yours, [23]and you are of Christ, and Christ is of God.

[a]19 Job 5:13   [b]20 Psalm 94:11   [c]22 That is, Peter

NOTES ON 1 CORINTHIANS 3:1-23

Summary ... Paul returns to the question of factions in the Corinthian Church. The problem is that by misunderstanding the nature of wisdom, by viewing the gospel as if it were just another philosophical system, by then exalting certain teachers into leaders of rival factions each with its own "philosophy," they betray their immaturity as Christians. Instead the Corinthian Christians need to understand that they are God's field and God's building; and that Paul, Apollos, and the others are mere servants who assist God in bringing about their growth and their molding into a Temple. By pretending to be "wise" (by the standards of the world) they show themselves to be "foolish" (in the eyes of God). They must stop exalting men, put an end to their divisions, and rest in the fact that "all things" are already theirs.

v. 1 **Brothers** ... Despite his criticism they are still part of the same family. The issue is not whether they are true Christians or not, but whether they are mature or immature in their faith.

spiritual ... A mature Christian whose life is dominated by the indwelling Spirit.

worldly ... Those Christians who are molded more by the spirit of the age than by the Spirit of God; those whose life and thoughts are so immature that they are "mere infants."

v. 2 **I gave you milk** ... Paul continues his metaphor. When he was in Corinth, they were not yet ready for "solid food."

still not ready ... To his disappointment, they are *still* immature, as evidenced by their factions.

v. 3 ... Jealousy and quarreling are clear indications that their lives are not controlled by the Spirit and that they are still "infants."

mere men ... Their lifestyle with its self-centered orientation ("*I* follow") is not in accord with that of the mature Christian. By exalting certain teachers they betray their lack of understanding of the gospel. Paul's point is that although they *have* the Spirit (and are therefore "spiritual" in the true sense), they are acting precisely like people *without* the Spirit. Chances are, given chapters 12-14, they thought rather highly of their own spirituality!

v. 5 **servants** ... Paul and Apollos are not to be exalted. They are merely servants, and not of very high order. (This same word was used to describe a waiter). They were simply carrying out the task God had called them to.

v. 6 **I planted** ... Paul was the first evangelist to preach in Corinth.

Apollos watered ... Apollos continued Paul's work by assisting in the building up of a new church.

God made it grow ... Still, their labors alone would not have been enough. The divine life-force necessary to produce growth came from God. This point is reiterated in verse 7.

v. 8 **one purpose** ... Paul and Apollos were colleagues, not rivals. They had the same ultimate purpose even though they had different specific tasks to fulfill (one began the work, the other nurtured it).

v. 9 **God's field** ... The Corinthians are the field which God is plowing via his servants.

God's building ... Paul shifts the metaphor now from agriculture to architecture.

vv. 10-17 ... Paul now develops his new metaphor of the church as a *structure* which God is building. Note that as in the previous metaphor, this one refers to the church as a whole and not to believers as individuals.

v. 10 **I laid the foundation** ... By preaching Christ, who is the foundation (v. 11), Paul was the one who began the work in Corinth (v. 6).

expert ... Literally "wise." Paul continues to develop the idea of wisdom.

builder ... (architekton). The one who plans and supervises the construction of a

---

GROUP AGENDA continued

your church which, because it is liturgical, he considers "worldly" and "dead." Yet to you this church has been a tremendous help. How would you reply to him based on this passage?

TO CLOSE/5-20 Minutes (Choose 1 or 2)

☐ What did you put down for APPLY? ☐ How would you describe yourself spiritually in a chronological term (infant, toddler, grade schooler, adolescent, etc.)? What is it going to take to move you to the next stage? ☐ Who was the person or persons that planted the "seed" in your spiritual life? Who "watered" it? ☐ In your own ministry, what seems to stand the test of "fire" and time? ☐ How do you feel about being God's "temple"?

building (not the one who does the actual labor).

v. 11 ... A community might be built on another foundation (e.g., the leadership and ideas of a famous philosopher) but it would not be the *Church*. The church's only foundation is the person of Jesus Christ (see 1:18-25).

v. 12 ... Paul describes some of the ways a person can go astray (as he warns in v. 10b) in building on the foundation— namely by using inferior or inadequate materials.

gold, silver, costly stones ... These materials will survive the test of fire.

wood, hay, or straw ... These will burn up.

v. 13 **The Day** ... On the Day of Judgment the quality of such labor will be revealed.

revealed with fire ... The idea is not of fire as punishment but of fire as a means of testing, a way of revealing the "quality of each man's work." This is a strong warning to those who lead the church.

v. 14 **reward** ... God's approval.

vv. 16-17 ... Paul extends his metaphor by pointing out that this is no ordinary building, but it is a temple that God is building. Their Christian community is a temple; i.e., the place where God lives and where he is therefore met and worshipped. The Church is the community within which the Spirit dwells.

v. 16 **temple** ... Paul tells them what kind of building they as a community are becoming (the reference is *not* to individual believer's bodies as the temple of the Spirit; that comes in 6:20). This would be a particularly vivid and exciting image for the Corinthians, surrounded as they were by a multitude of pagan temples, because Paul shows them that within their community—wherever it gathered—God's Spirit was at work creating a new people.

v. 17 **destroy** ... The idea has shifted from losing one's pay for having used inferior building materials (vv. 12-15) to being punished for destroying the church. If the Corinthians continue quarreling instead of accepting the leadership of God's Spirit, they defile his holy temple and are therefore marked for destruction.

sacred ... It is special, set apart to God.

v. 18-23 ... Paul concludes his discussion of wisdom and folly; though he will later refer back to it (e.g., 6:5; 8:1f; 10:15; 12:8; 13:8-12) and brings to an end, as well, his comments on their divisions.

v. 18 **do not deceive yourselves** ... "Self-deception is the common fate of those who mistakenly fancy themselves wise; deluded in this, they are deluded in many other matters ... They estimate wisdom by the wrong standards. Such men need to take new standards and reverse their judgments" (Barrett).

become a "fool" ... Should a person deem him/herself "wise" in terms of prevailing standards (i.e., "wisdom of the world") it is not possible to become "wise" in God's ways without first turning from the old wisdom (repenting) and then opening oneself up to the Holy Spirit who brings the new (spiritual) wisdom.

v. 19 ... The simple fact is that God's wisdom and the wisdom of the world are at opposite poles. From God's perspective what the world calls "wisdom" is really "foolishness."

"He catches the wise in their craftiness" ... "The *wise* are like cunning beasts for whom the hunter is nevertheless too clever." (Barrett)

v. 20 **thoughts** ... The plans and philosophies of people.

vain ... Futile, ineffectual.

v. 21 **no more boasting about men!** ... In the light of all this, Paul calls upon them to bring to an end their divisions.

All things are yours ... Rather than spending their time pitting one leader against another, Paul would have the Corinthians remember that leaders and people are all servants of Christ destined to be sovereign over all creation. It is not that Christians control in a manipulative sense, the *world, life, death, the present and the future.* The point is that no longer do these have final power over them (Romans 8:38f). Ultimately, since they are Christ's and *Christ is of God* (v. 23), the church will experience triumph over what once dominated it. In the face of such an amazing truth, it is absurd to continue their petty divisions!

UNIT 6—Apostles of Christ/1 Corinthians 4:1-21

TEXT

Apostles of Christ

4 So then, men ought to regard us as servants of Christ and as those entrusted with the secret things of God. ²Now it is required that those who have been given a trust must prove faithful. ³I care very little if I am judged by you or by any human court; indeed, I do not even judge myself. ⁴My conscience is clear, but that does not make me innocent. It is the Lord who judges me. ⁵Therefore judge nothing before the appointed time; wait till the Lord comes. He will bring to light what is hidden in darkness and will expose the motives of men's hearts. At that time each will receive his praise from God.

⁶Now, brothers, I have applied these things to myself and Apollos for your benefit, so that you may learn from us the meaning of the saying, "Do not go beyond what is written." Then you will not take pride in one man over against another. ⁷For who makes you different from anyone else? What do you have that you did not receive? And if you did receive it, why do you boast as though you did not?

⁸Already you have all you want! Already you have become rich! You have become kings—and that without us! How I wish that you really had become kings so that we might be kings with you! ⁹For it seems to me that God has put us apostles on display at the end of the procession, like men condemned to die in the arena. We have been made a spectacle to the whole universe, to angels as well as to men. ¹⁰We are fools for Christ, but you are so wise in Christ! We are weak, but you are strong! You are honored, we are dishonored! ¹¹To this very hour we go hungry and thirsty, we are in rags, we are brutally treated, we are homeless. ¹²We work hard with our own hands. When we are cursed, we bless; when we are persecuted, we endure it; ¹³when we are slandered, we answer kindly. Up to this moment we have become the

Continued on next page

STUDY

READ

First Reading/First Impressions

I think here that Paul is . . . ☐ angry. ☐ boasting. ☐ complaining. ☐ being ironic. ☐ putting these people down. ☐ putting these people in their place. ☐ giving them an example to follow.

Second Reading/Big Idea

With what tone of voice do you imagine Paul speaking in verses 1-7? 8-13? 14-21?

SEARCH

1. What does Paul's reminder in verse 1 reveal about what was going on in this church?

2. Although faithfulness is required in a leader, what is revealed about some people's view of Paul? (vv. 3-5)

3. How does Paul deal with this suspicion? (vv. 3-5)

4. Given the context of this situation (where factions of the church judge one another on the basis of the reputation of the leader they follow), what do you think Paul means by the proverb in verse 6?

5. How was this pride in their leaders really a form of pride in themselves? (v. 7)

6. What "attitude problem" in this church lies behind Paul's irony in verses 8 and 10? (see also v. 18)

7. In contrast to the self-centered, "power-oriented" message some of the Corinthians believed, what does Paul's example of life as an apostle (vv. 9-13) reveal about real Christianity?

8. In verses 16-17 he wants them to imitate his way of life. How does this square with his admonition not to be a follower of one leader or another through chapters 1-3?

APPLY

Who is one Christian today that you admire for putting his or her faith on the line? (e.g., Archbishop Desmond Tutu, Mother Theresa, Billy Graham, or maybe some "lesser known" believer who is faithful in hard times)

What is one quality in his or her life that you want to "imitate"?

"You can have it all." This is the promise of a popular beer commercial. You can have complete control over your life. What would the apostle Paul say about this—based on verses 8-13? Rephrase Paul's philosophy of life in a few words in the box below. Then put an "X" someplace between these two statements to indicate where you stand between these two philosophies.

"You can have it all."

GROUP AGENDA

Divide into groups of 4 before you start to share. And follow the time recommendations.

TO BEGIN/10 Minutes (Choose 1 or 2)

☐ Were you ever sent to the principal's office or paddled in school? ☐ In your family, who gave you a "good talking to" when you needed it? ☐ As a child, what was one time you felt totally embarrassed at school? ☐ do you see yourself more as a "dreamer of dreams" or a "doer of deeds"? Why? ☐ What did you jot down for your "first impressions" under READ?

TO GO DEEPER/20 Minutes (Choose 2 or 3)

☐ Share your SEARCH portion of the Bible study first—one person answering the first question, the next person the next, etc. ☐ From the sound of it, what do you think was going on in the church to occasion this lecture from

Continued on next page

---

scum of the earth, the refuse of the world. ¹⁴I am not writing this to shame you, but to warn you, as my dear children. ¹⁵Even though you have ten thousand guardians in Christ, you do not have many fathers, for in Christ Jesus I became your father, through the gospel. ¹⁶Therefore I urge you to imitate me. ¹⁷For this reason I am sending to you Timothy, my son whom I love, who is faithful in the Lord. He will remind you of my way of life in Christ Jesus, which agrees with what I teach everywhere in every church.

¹⁸Some of you have become arrogant, as if I were not coming to you. ¹⁹But I will come to you very soon, if the Lord is willing, and then I will find out not only how these arrogant people are talking, but what power they have. ²⁰For the kingdom of God is not a matter of talk but of power. ²¹What do you prefer? Shall I come to you with a whip, or in love and with a gentle spirit?

NOTES ON 1 CORINTHIANS 4:1-21

Summary: Chapter 3 seemed a fitting close to Paul's discussion about divisiveness. But in chapter 4 he has one thing more to do. He must reassert his authority as an apostle over the church (so he can deal with the problems there). Yet he must do so without negating what he just said about the value of the work of other leaders like Apollos. In chapter 4 he will assert his special authority by reminding them of the role he played in their spiritual life. He is their spiritual father.

v. 1 **So then** . . . Paul draws his conclusions from what he has just taught.

men ought to regard us . . . his topic is how Christians should relate to their ministers.

GROUP AGENDA continued
Paul? If you had been one of those responsible for this conduct in the church, how would you have felt after getting this letter? ☐ What is the "procession" in verse 9 alluding to? ☐ In what sense is Paul a "fool" for Christ? ☐ Case History: "If you give your life to Christ, God will make you a success." This is what the preacher said when Bill turned over his life to Christ. But the opposite has happened. He lost his job, his home, and his wife is very sick. He comes to you for counsel.

TO CLOSE/5-20 Minutes (Choose 1 or 2)

☐ Share what you put down for APPLY in the Bible study. In light of what Paul says in verses 10-13, how should we respond to the idea popular in some circles today that "God wants you to be happy, rich, and successful?" ☐ Are you more likely to err on the side of honoring yourself or dishonoring yourself? What does a healthy balance look like? ☐ If Paul were to come to your group, would he come "with a whip, or in love and with a gentle spirit"? What would make the difference?

servants . . . First and foremost, a minister is a servant of Christ; under Christ's authority, at work on the task given him/her by Christ.

those entrusted . . . literally *stewards;* in a Greek household this was the slave who administered all the affairs of the family; i.e., he directed the staff, saw to securing supplies and, in effect, ran the whole household for his master.

secret things of God . . . As in 2:7, these are the plans of God once known only to himself but now revealed to all. The minister is, therefore, charged with preaching the gospel; it is his/her task to make known these mysteries.

v. 2 **faithful** . . . The key requirement for a steward is that he prove reliable in looking after his master's affairs, that he show himself to be trustworthy. But the question is: who will decide if the steward has been faithful? Paul answers this in verse 3.

vv. 3-4 . . . In fact, neither the Corinthians nor he himself is fit to rule upon his faithfulness as a steward of God. God is the only judge of that and Paul is content to rest in that knowledge and not let the criticism bother him.

v. 3 **judged by you** . . . As becomes evident, especially in 2 Corinthians, the Corinthians were very critical of Paul.

I do not even judge myself . . . " 'A good conscience is an invention of the devil.' Paul has one, but sets no store by it." (Barrett)

v. 4 **innocent** . . . Though Paul has no secret guilt, this is not a sign of innocence as much as of ignorance. Justification comes not because of innocence (no one is without sin) but by grace as a result of Christ's atoning death.

v. 5 **till the Lord comes** . . . At the second coming of Christ, the Day of Judgment will occur. Paul cautions about making premature judgments. Let the Lord judge. He is the only one able to do it properly since he alone can see not only a person's actions but that person's motives.

motives . . . Not just actions, but the very inward intentions will be made plain then.

v. 6 **do not take pride in one man** . . . As Paul has shown, he and Apollos are colleagues, servants of the same Christ, who have been given slightly different tasks but with the same overall purpose; so it is silly to set one against the other. To do this is clearly a matter of *pride* ("My leader is better than your leader and so I am better than you").

v. 7 . . . The antidote to pride is the recognition that all one has was received as a gift. Whatever spiritual gifts or virtues they might possess have come from God.

vv. 8-10 . . . Paul shifts to irony, perhaps parodying what was actually being said, in all seriousness, in Corinth.

v. 8a **already** . . . The Corinthians are acting as if the New Age had already been consummated and that they had come into the fullness of God, into their inheritance as children of God, and into the kingdom of God itself.

v. 8b **that we might be kings with you** . . . Paul wishes they were right because, in fact, his present experience was quite grim (vv. 11-12; 2 Corinthians 6:4-10).

v. 9 **the arena** . . . The image is of the triumphal return of a Roman general who parades his trophies before the people. At the end of the procession marches a band of captives who will be taken into the arena to fight and die.

v. 10 **fools for Christ** . . . By the standards of the world's wisdom Paul is indeed foolish. Still, as he has already shown (3:18), this is the pathway to God's wisdom.

you are so wise in Christ . . . In ironic contrast Paul points out that the Corinthians, in their worldly wisdom, are acting as if they were wise and superior.

we are weak . . . In fact, in God's economy, weakness is strength. Christ came not as a mighty conquering hero but to be crucified as a common criminal. In the suffering Savior one finds the model for the Christian life. See 2 Corinthians 12:9; 13:4.

vv. 11-12 . . . The irony drops away and Paul relates what it is really like to be an apostle.

v. 11 **hungry, thirsty, in rags** . . . The long journeys which the apostles undertook were not easy. They were characterized by deprivation of all sorts, by lack of supplies, by robbery, and by general hardships.

treated badly . . . The phrase describes the treatment given a slave; they are beaten up in a demeaning fashion as if they were nothing.

homeless . . . The constant travel left them without a home.

v. 12 **we work hard** . . . As Paul did in Corinth making tents with Priscilla and Aquila (see Acts 18:3; 20:34).

vv. 12b-13a . . . The apostles seek to live out the principles in the Sermon on the Mount.

v. 13 **the scum of the earth** . . . The word *scum* refers to the dirt and filth removed in cleaning; such a task was given to the most worthless people and so to be called this was a derogatory slur.

vv. 14-21 . . . Paul ends the section begun in 1:10. Their preference for worldly wisdom has led them to develop "an arrogant attitude in which (perhaps subconsciously) they patronized their missionaries and ministers and attempted to play them off against one another. Paul's answer is in a theology and a way of life rooted in the cross" (Barrett). By means of the metaphor of a father with his children Paul reasserts his authority over the Corinthian Church and so prepares to deal with their aberrant behavior.

v. 14 **to shame you** . . . Indeed, any Corinthian ought to be blushing in acute distress at this point over what he/she had become and at how far he/she had departed from Christ's intentions. Still, it is not *shame* Paul intends.

warn . . . The word means "to admonish" as a father might do, in hopes that his children will see the error of their ways and change.

v. 15 **guardians** . . . Tutors, Christian leaders who instruct them in the faith (3:6, 8, 10).

your father . . . Paul led them to faith in Christ.

v. 16 **imitate me** . . . If, in fact, they need a model of how to live the Christian life (and it is clear that on their own they are not doing too well), they can look to Paul. In him they would see a servant eager to do Christ's bidding and a man willing to walk in the steps of a despised, crucified Savior (vv. 11-12). See Galatians 4:12; Philippians 3:17; 1 Thessalonians 1:6, 2:14; 2 Thessalonians 3:7, 9.

v. 17 **For this reason** . . . Because Paul wishes them to imitate his lifestyle and because he himself cannot come yet (though he is planning a trip), he will send Timothy who will model for them the Christian lifestyle.

my son . . . Timothy was a convert of Paul's.

v. 18 **as if I were not coming** . . . While Paul was in Corinth he restrained the situation. But now in his absence it seems that some have turned their freedom in Christ into license.

v. 20 **kingdom of God** . . . The reign of God which is already here but not yet in fullness.

not a matter of talk but of power . . . It is one thing to make loud boasts and claim great wisdom. It is quite another to live out the power of God.

UNIT 7—Expel the Immoral Brother/1 Corinthians 5:1-13

TEXT

Expel the Immoral Brother!

5 It is actually reported that there is sexual immorality among you, and of a kind that does not occur even among pagans: A man has his father's wife. ²And you are proud! Shouldn't you rather have been filled with grief and have put out of your fellowship the man who did this? ³Even though I am not physically present, I am with you in spirit. And I have already passed judgment on the one who did this, just as if I were present. ⁴When you are assembled in the name of our Lord Jesus and I am with you in spirit, and the power of our Lord Jesus is present, ⁵hand this man over to Satan, so that the sinful nature[a] may be destroyed and his spirit saved on the day of the Lord.

⁶Your boasting is not good. Don't you know that a little yeast works through the whole batch of dough? ⁷Get rid of the old yeast that you may be a new batch without yeast—as you really are. For Christ, our Passover lamb, has been sacrificed. ⁸Therefore let us keep the Festival, not with the old yeast, the yeast of malice and wickedness, but with bread without yeast, the bread of sincerity and truth.

⁹I have written you in my letter not to associate with sexually immoral people—¹⁰not at all meaning the people of this world who are immoral, or the greedy and swindlers, or idolaters. In that case you would have to leave this world. ¹¹But now I am writing you that you must not associate with anyone who calls himself a brother but is sexually immoral or greedy, an idolater or a slanderer, a drunkard or a swindler. With such a man do not even eat.

¹²What business is it of mine to judge those outside the church? Are you not to judge those inside? ¹³God will judge those outside. "Expel the wicked man from among you."[b]

[a]5 Or *that his body; or that the flesh*   [b]13 Deut. 17:7; 19:19; 22:21, 24; 24:7

STUDY

READ

First Reading/First Impressions
As the editor of the "Corinthian Enquirer" again, what juicy headline would you come up with for this situation?

Second Reading/Big Idea
In spite of the "sensational" nature of this situation, what verse highlights the main concern for Paul?

SEARCH

1. Although the facts of this situation are unclear to us (e.g., was the man's father still alive . . . and still married to the woman? Or was the man married to this woman, or co-habiting, or just having sex with her occasionally?), Paul is angry that the Corinthians are "proud" and "boastful" of this situation (vv. 2, 6). What might he mean by that? ☐ They are happy for the man. ☐ They think this is a legitimate expression of Christian freedom. ☐ They take pleasure in pushing back traditional standards. ☐ They just don't see it as a problem. ☐ _____ Why?

2. How would you paraphrase what Paul tells them to do about this situation? (vv. 4-5)

3. If you were a Corinthian church member, how would you explain to your next door (pagan) neighbor why this man had been expelled? (v. 5)

4. From the yeast imagery (vv. 6-8), what is Paul's concern if this situation is allowed to go on without discipline?

5. How is this consistent with the "new bread" they have become through Christ's sacrifice? (vv. 7-8)

6. How is the way a Christian relates to those outside the faith to be different than the way he or she relates to those professing faith? (vv. 9-11) Why?

APPLY

Compare this passage with Matthew 18:15-17, 1 John 5:16, 2 Corinthians 2:5-8, and Galatians 6:1-2. From these passages, write out a summary of the spirit, mechanics, and purpose of church discipline.

In your situation, do you tend to be overly judgmental of others or too permissive? Why?

GROUP AGENDA

Divide into groups of 4 before you start to share. And follow the time recommendations.

TO BEGIN/10 Minutes (Choose 1 or 2)

☐ When you were a child, what was the group that you ran around with (this can be an informal or more formal group)? ☐ What feelings does the word "expel" bring to mind? ☐ Did your parents ever forbid you to associate with someone? How did you feel at the time? How do you feel about this now? Did any parents ever forbid their children to associate with you? How did you feel about that? ☐ What did you put down for READ in the Bible study?

TO GO DEEPER/20 Minutes (Choose 2 or 3)

☐ Share your Bible study under SEARCH first. ☐ From what is said in this passage, what do you think was going on in the church in Corinth? ☐ What does it mean to "hand over to Satan"? How do you reconcile Paul's teaching here with that in 4:3-5? What is the point in each? ☐ What is the spiritual principle in this passage on church discipline? Do you feel this principle still applies today? ☐ Case History: A man and a woman start coming to your church and like it. They love each other and have lived together for a year, yet are not married because the woman just wants some time to heal the emotional scars incurred by her failed marriage previously. How do you relate to them?

TO CLOSE/5-20 Minutes (Choose 1 or 2)

☐ What did you put down for your position on spiritual discipline? ☐ Can you think of a time when you wish the church would have disciplined you? ☐ What spirit or attitude must be present in the person or group administering discipline for you to accept it? ☐ What would happen if the church took this passage seriously?

NOTES ON 1 CORINTHIANS 5:1-13

Summary ... Paul now tackles the second problem which has been reported to him: incest in the church. One of the members is sexually involved with his father's wife. Paul is concerned not just with this sin itself, but also with the reaction of the Corinthians to it. Instead of grieving over what has happened, they rather arrogantly accept the whole situation and do not discipline the man by putting him out of the church.

v. 1 **sexual immorality** ... Literally "fornication." Since Paul does not label this "adultery," the man's father was probably either dead or divorced from his wife. For newly-converted pagans, this whole question of the relationship between the sexes was especially troublesome since the environment out of which they had been converted was notoriously lax when it came to sexual standards.

even among pagans ... It was not that incest had never been practiced by pagans. Paul's point is that incest was also condemned by pagans (as well as by Jews: Leviticus 18:8; 20:11). Both Jew and Gentile were aghast at the idea of a father and a son having sexual relations with the same woman.

has ... By this verb Paul indicates that the man in question was not just involved casually with this woman but was indeed living with her.

his father's wife ... The way Paul has phrased this indicates that she was probably not the man's actual mother, but rather his stepmother. Furthermore, she is probably not a Christian since Paul does not refer to her again. He only recommends discipline for the man (see vv. 12-13).

v. 2 **you are proud** ... Paul may mean that they are proud *because* of the situation (it demonstrates their tolerance and their freedom. They are so "spiritual" they do not have to worry about "bodily" sins); or he may mean that they are proud *in spite of* such a situation, even though this of all things ought to have burst the bubble of their arrogance ("proud" is literally "puffed up").

shouldn't you rather ... Paul points out that what they should have *felt* was grief (how could they be proud when such a thing was going on) and what they should have *done* was to discipline the offender.

grief ... Literally "mourning"; their emotional response to what this man was doing ought to be the same as if he had died.

vv. 4-6 ... Paul is quite clear about what ought to be done. The church must meet together and formally exclude the erring member from its fellowship; not so much as a punitive measure, but in order that on the Day of Judgment his spirit might be saved. The aim of this action is salvation, not destruction.

v. 5 ... "The thought may be that the devil must be given his due, but can claim no more; if he has the flesh, he has no right to the spirit, even of the sinner. The thought may be simply that of 3:15: the man's essential self will be saved with the loss not only of his work but of his flesh" (Barrett).

when you are assembled ... Such excommunication is done not by Paul nor by the leaders of the church but by the *whole* church, gathered together in the power of Jesus.

hand the man over to Satan ... "To be excluded from the sphere in which Christ's work was operative was to be thrust back into that in which Satan still exercised authority ... This authority, however, was limited. If a man was handed over to Satan it was not that Satan might have his way with him, but with a view to his ultimate salvation. Satan, in fact, was being used as a tool in the intents of Christ and the church" (Barrett).

that the sinful nature may be destroyed ... It is not clear what Paul has in mind here, though probably he does not envision the man's death. Instead he hopes that by exclusion from the church he may see clearly the enormity of his loss and so repent of his sin and return (see 1 Timothy 1:20).

vv. 6-8 ... While Paul's first concern is for the ultimate welfare of the erring brother (vv. 4-6), he is also concerned about the welfare of the church. He uses first the image of yeast as a corrupting agent and then refers to the (related) idea of the Passover.

v. 6 **yeast** ... This word is literally "leaven," i.e., a piece of dough which had been kept out from the previous baking. This dough then fermented and was used in the next batch of bread to cause it to rise. Jews associated fermenting with rotting and so leaven became a symbol of evil. On the day before the Passover Feast all the old

COMMENTS

leaven was tossed out of the house as a symbol of cleansing and purification—an apt image, given the situation in the Corinthian Church.

the whole batch ... Paul's point is that just as a small amount of yeast penetrates the whole batch of dough, so too one member given over to this sort of gross evil will affect the whole church and corrupt it. Just as leaven is tossed out prior to Passover, so too this evil must be put out of the church.

v. 7 **get rid of ... that you may be** ... As he often does, here Paul speaks in the indicative ("Do this") and then the imperative ("Be what you already are"). Christians have been set free from the bondage of sin, and so they must live out this reality in their daily lives. Both the indicative and the imperative are vital. "The imperative is unthinkable without the indicative, which makes the otherwise impossible obedience possible; the indicative is emasculated if the imperative, which gives it moral bite, is wanting" (Barrett).

Passover ... The Jewish Festival celebrating the deliverance of Israel out of Egypt during which lambs were sacrificed in the Temple as an offering for sin (see Exodus 12:1-36). Christ became the final and ultimate sin offering. Thus Christians have been freed from sin and so must avoid sin.

v. 9 **I have written** ... Paul refers to a previous (and now lost) letter which he had written to them.

Incest Laws

Originally incest laws were developed in order to define who was too closely related to be married. Incest laws were designed to prevent intramarriage. Law alone, of course, was insufficient to prevent such things from happening, and so the Bible records instances of incest: Genesis 19:30-36; 35:22; 49:1-4; 2 Samuel 13:1-22; Ezekiel 22:10-11; as well as 1 Corinthians 5.

The laws regulating marriage are found primarily in the Pentateuch. In Leviticus 18:6-16 sexual intercourse is prohibited with the following women: one's mother or any other wife of one's father (this was the prohibition violated in Corinth); a sister; the daughter of a son or daughter; the daughter of the father's wife; the sister of one's father or mother; an aunt; a daughter-in-law, or a sister-in-law. Deuteronomy 27:23 adds that one is not allowed to marry one's mother-in-law. The penalty for breaking such prohibitions is childlessness (Leviticus 20:21) or death (Leviticus 20:11-13). Such offenders were ordered to be "cut off from their people" (Leviticus 18:29). To be without tribe or family was an especially odious penalty in Old Testament times. The severity of the penalties indicates the seriousness with which this offense was regarded.

It seems that all societies have some form of taboo against incest. The reply by an Arapesh (a New Guinea tribesman) to Margaret Mead (the anthropologist) sheds an interesting insight on the social and economic implications of intramarriage:

> What, you would like to marry your sister! What is the matter with you any way? Don't you want a brother-in-law? Don't you realize that if you marry another man's sister and another man marries your sister, you will have at least two brothers-in-law, while if you marry your own sister you will have none? With whom will you hunt, with whom will you garden, whom will you go to visit?

v. 10 ... Paul makes it quite plain that he is *not* calling for total withdrawal from the world into an exclusive cult-like existence.

v. 11 ... On the other hand, he does call for withdrawal *from fellow Christians* who are involved in open sin.

do not even eat ... This is the practical outworking of excommunication. All contact is severed.

v. 12 **judge those inside** ... The aim of such judgment is not punitive but redemptive; Paul is calling for discipline, not punishment.

v. 13 **God will judge** ... On the last day.

"Expel the wicked ..." ... For the fifth time (see also vv. 2, 5, 7, 11) Paul tells them to excommunicate this man, here quoting from the Old Testament. At times drastic measures are necessary to safeguard the body of Christ. This was especially true as the new church in Corinth faced pressures from paganism which threatened to corrupt it into something quite different from what God intended.

UNIT 8—Lawsuits Among Believers/1 Corinthians 6:1-11

TEXT

Lawsuits Among Believers

6 If any of you has a dispute with another, dare he take it before the ungodly for judgment instead of before the saints? ²Do you not know that the saints will judge the world? And if you are to judge the world, are you not competent to judge trivial cases? ³Do you not know that we will judge angels? How much more the things of this life! ⁴Therefore, if you have disputes about such matters, appoint as judges even men of little account in the church!ᵃ ⁵I say this to shame you. Is it possible that there is nobody among you wise enough to judge a dispute between believers? ⁶But instead, one brother goes to law against another—and this in front of unbelievers!

⁷The very fact that you have lawsuits among you means you have been completely defeated already. Why not rather be wronged? Why not rather be cheated? ⁸Instead, you yourselves cheat and do wrong, and you do this to your brothers.

⁹Do you not know that the wicked will not inherit the kingdom of God? Do not be deceived: Neither the sexually immoral nor idolaters nor adulterers nor male prostitutes nor homosexual offenders ¹⁰nor thieves nor the greedy nor drunkards nor slanderers nor swindlers will inherit the kingdom of God. ¹¹And that is what some of you were. But you were washed, you were sanctified, you were justified in the name of the Lord Jesus Christ and by the Spirit of our God.

[a] 4 Or *matters, do you appoint as judges men of little account in the church?*

STUDY

READ

First Reading/First Impressions

If you were in this church, what would you feel when you read this part of the letter? ☐ Paul is a meddler. ☐ Oh, I wish he hadn't heard of this. ☐ What happens when the leaders do wrong?

Second Reading/Big Idea

What seems to be Paul's biggest concern here?

SEARCH

1. Both from what is stated and reading "between the lines," what reasons are behind Paul's shock over these Christians bringing lawsuits against one another?

(v. 2)

(v. 3)

(vv. 5-6)

2. Since the church would have no legal power, how would the alternative he offers possibly work? (v. 4)

3. What does Paul see as the real problem? (vv. 7-8)

4. Do you think this is primarily a call to let injustice continue? Or to not seek revenge under the guise of "justice"? Or a rebuke over the fact that they not only complain about injustice but commit it? Why?

5. What does Paul mean by his statement in verses 9-10? That anyone who has done these things cannot be saved? That a lifestyle marked by these things is proof that a person is not a Christian? That indulging in these things without a sense of remorse shows that a person is not a Christian? Why?

6. How does Paul's reminder of their status in Christ (v. 11) relate to the rest of this passage?

APPLY

What attitudes underlying this situation do you see in yourself at times?

- ☐ An insistence on "my rights" as my first priority.
- ☐ More of a desire to get back at people rather than to make things right with them.
- ☐ A willingness to "bend the rules" a bit if it helps me get ahead (and no one notices).
- ☐ Forgetting to consider how my relationship with Christ is to affect other relationships.
- ☐ Wanting to hold on to my old way of life rather than really changing to follow Christ.

What is one thing you could do this week to work on changing these attitudes?

What will you ask the group to help you with as you seek to change these attitudes? (Pray for a specific situation, ask me next week how I did, etc.)

GROUP AGENDA

Divide into groups of 4 before you start to share and follow the time recommendations.

TO BEGIN/10 Minutes (Choose 1 or 2)

How did your parents settle disputes between you and your brother or sister when you were kids? Did you ever feel like you were unfairly treated by the arbitrator? ☐ What was the greatest wrong you felt someone did to you when you were a kid? How did you respond? How did you *want* to respond? ☐ When, if ever, have you had an experience with a judge? How did you feel about it? ☐ What did you jot down under READ?

TO GO DEEPER/20 Minutes (Choose 2 or 3)

Share the results of the Bible study—one person taking question 1, the next person taking question 2, etc. ☐ What, in your own words, is the position in this Scripture about nonretaliation when we are wronged? ☐ Case History: In 1987, an investigation by a major denomination found out that in many churches, the church treasurer was skimming money from the offering. From your study, what recommendations for action would you give to deal with such situations? ☐ Where does this passage draw the line between standing up for "our rights" and giving up "our rights"?

TO CLOSE/5-20 Minutes (Choose 1 or 2)

What did you put down for APPLY in the Bible study? ☐ What was the last dispute you had with a fellow Christian? How did the two of you resolve it? What did you learn from this encounter? ☐ How do you usually handle wrongs done to you? Do you agree with Paul that it's better to be cheated than to go to court with a believer? ☐ What does it *feel like* to be washed, sanctified and justified? What, if anything, does it make you want to do?

NOTES ON 1 CORINTHIANS 6:1-11

Summary ... Paul's concern in chapter 5 is not just with the particular case he has noted. He is even more concerned with the congregation's need to exercise self-discipline. In chapter 6 he cites a second example of their failure to deal with internal disorder. The church has not dealt adequately with disputes between members over financial matters. Instead Christians are suing one another in secular courts. This is wrong, Paul says. The church needs to learn that it must "judge those inside" the church (5:12). Paul says two things in chapter 6 in response to this specific problem. First, Christians—of all people—ought to be able to settle their own disputes (vv. 1-6); and second, in any case they ought not to be at odds with one another (vv. 7-11).

v. 1 ... The Jewish community settled its disputes internally as did certain pagan religious groups. Of all people, those who are one day destined to judge the world ought to be able to manage their own conflicts without recourse to the secular court.

dare he ... The implication is that such action is an affront to God and to the church.

the ungodly ... This is not used in a pejorative sense to indicate that Roman judges were unfair. It was at Corinth that Paul experienced for himself the impartiality of Roman justice (Acts 18:12-17). Here this term simply means "non-Christian."

for judgment ... The bench from which justice was dispensed was located out in the open in Corinth—in the market place; which is perhaps one reason why Paul was so upset. In hauling a brother or sister into court, a Christian was not simply settling a dispute. He/she was also holding the church itself up to public scrutiny and ridicule. This is another instance in which new Christians brought into the church old patterns of life. The Greeks were notorious for going to court. The law court seemed to be one of their chief amusements.

saints ... This can hardly be taken as an assessment of the high moral standards of these church members since in going to court they are clearly acting in an unacceptable fashion. Here the term simply means "Christians."

v. 2 **judge the world** ... In some way or another, on the Day of Judgment, Christians will assist in the process of judgment. Paul's point here stands in contrast to 5:12 where he says Christians are not to be judgmental (censorious) toward the non-Christian *in the here and now.*

trivial ... Though the person bringing the suit might not feel it to be so, in contrast to the sort of judgment Christians will be involved in on the Last Day (judging the world and angels), these matters are quite insignificant.

v. 3 **judge angels** ... There are both good and bad angels, and even though *angels* are the highest form of created being, Christians will judge them.

v. 5 **to shame you** ... In contrast to 4:14, here Paul does use shame as a way to bring the Corinthians to their senses.

wise enough ... If they are really as wise as they claim (this is their point of pride—see 1:18-2:16) then surely they ought to be able to settle internal disputes.

v. 6 ... "A church has come to a pretty pass when its members believe that they are more likely to get justice from *unbelievers* than from their own brothers" (Barrett).

v. 7 ... Having completed his general instructions to the church about lawsuits, Paul now addresses his words to the individual who brought the lawsuit in the first place.

defeated already ... The very fact of a lawsuit is a clear sign that in the church love has been replaced by selfishness.

Why not rather be wronged? ... Paul counsels nonretaliation, as Jesus had taught (Matthew 5:38-42, see also Romans 12:17-21; 1 Thessalonians 5:15). Such a stance is only possible because the Christian knows that his/her true life is to be found in the coming New Age. "He can suffer wrong in the *already,* precisely because his life is conditioned by the future. That is, he has been set free from the tyranny of the selfishness that dominates the present age. He is free to live out the life of love that characterizes the age to come. He is free to do this because in Christ he has died and has been raised to live in the new age" (Fee).

v. 8 ... Paul now turns to the offending person who started the whole affair by cheating (or wronging somehow) another Christian.

vv. 9-11 . . . Paul warns the whole church that they must live out in reality what in fact is true of them. They have been transformed and so they must put behind the "old ways" (like defrauding one another).

v. 9 **wicked** . . . Paul is thinking of those who actively live out a life of evil. He then illustrates what he means by the list that follows in which he points to typical destructive lifestyles in Corinth and elsewhere in the Graeco-Roman world. These were the patterns of life that the Corinthians had to resist and put behind them, though the temptation to bring these into the church was very strong as is seen in chapters 5 and 6.

kingdom of God . . . Paul continues with this idea of living out the ethic of the Age to Come, referring here to the time when all evil is undone and God reigns visibly.

male prostitutes nor homosexual offenders . . . The passive and active partners in male homosexual activity. Homosexuality was widespread in the Graeco-Roman world; 14 of the first 15 Roman emperors practiced it.

v. 10 **thieves** . . . The typical target of thieves was clothing which they stole from the public bath house or the public gymnasium. Homes were also easy to break into.

v. 11 **That is what some of you were** . . . Paul is not saying that such offenders are beyond redemption. On the contrary, one senses here his wonder and amazement at the fact that God can and does transform lives, even those who practiced such gross evil.

you were washed . . . This transformation of life begins with the inner cleansing from sin (which later was symbolized by the outward act of baptism).

sanctified . . . Paul probably is not thinking of the process whereby a Christian grows in grace since this word precedes justification in the list. Rather the idea is of having been made a *saint*, i.e., one of God's own family.

justified . . . Acquitted from the consequences of sin because Christ took the penalty on himself. "Paul is not saying that the Corinthians have been made good men, perfectly holy and righteous; it is evident from the context that they have a long way to travel along the road of moral virtue. He claims that, gross as their sins have been, they have for Christ's sake been freed from guilt, united to God, and acquitted" (Barrett).

UNIT 9—Sexual Immorality/1 Corinthians 6:12-20

TEXT

Sexual Immorality

¹²"Everything is permissible for me"—but not everything is beneficial. "Everything is permissible for me"—but I will not be mastered by anything. ¹³"Food for the stomach and the stomach for food"—but God will destroy them both. The body is not meant for sexual immorality, but for the Lord, and the Lord for the body. ¹⁴By his power God raised the Lord from the dead, and he will raise us also. ¹⁵Do you not know that your bodies are members of Christ himself? Shall I then take the members of Christ and unite them with a prostitute? Never! ¹⁶Do you not know that he who unites himself with a prostitute is one with her in body? For it is said, "The two will become one flesh."[a] ¹⁷But he who unites himself with the Lord is one with him in spirit.

¹⁸Flee from sexual immorality. All other sins a man commits are outside his body, but he who sins sexually sins against his own body. ¹⁹Do you not know that your body is a temple of the Holy Spirit, who is in you, whom you have received from God? You are not your own; ²⁰you were bought at a price. Therefore honor God with your body.

[a]16 Gen. 2:24

STUDY

READ

First Reading/First Impressions

"Corinthian Enquirer" time again . . . what would be your headline as you discovered what was going on here?

Second Reading/Big Idea

In your own words, write out what you think is the most important verse in this passage.

SEARCH

1. Compare the quotes in verse 12 with Galatians 5:1, 13a. From what you have already seen in this letter, how might the Corinthians have taken Paul's teaching about freedom in Christ and distorted it?

2. Without denying the reality of freedom in Christ, how would you describe what he means by the two ways he qualifies it in verse 12?

3. The quote in verse 13 reflects Paul's attitude toward the Jewish dietary laws (see Romans 14:14a). In a sentence or two, write out how it appears the Corinthians have applied that principle to sex.

4. To what principles does Paul appeal in arguing against their approach to casual sex?

(v. 13b)

(v. 14)

(v. 15)

(vv. 16-17)

(v. 18)

(vv. 19-20)

APPLY

Which of the above principles is most compelling to you? Why?

What is one area where you struggle between what is "permissible" and what is "beneficial"?

What is one specific way you want to begin a "temple maintenance program" (vv. 19-20) in regard to that struggle?

Write out verses 19-20 on a card and place it where you will see it regularly this week (over the sink, on the dashboard, etc.). Over the next week, memorize it. It will come in handy the rest of your life!

"Do you not know that your body is a temple of the Holy Spirit, who is in you, whom you have received from God? You are not your own; you were bought at a price. Therefore honor God with your body."
1 Corinthians 6:19-20 NIV

GROUP AGENDA

Divide into groups of 4 before you start to share and follow the time recommendations.

TO BEGIN/10 Minutes (Choose 1 or 2)

☐ What is one of the most impressive church buildings (or cathedrals) you have ever seen? What feelings did it create in you? ☐ What, if anything, did you dislike about your body when you were a teenager? When do you feel the best about your body? ☐ What did you put down in the Bible study after READ?

TO GO DEEPER/20 Minutes (Choose 2 or 3)

Share the SEARCH questions in the Bible study, one question at a time. ☐ Do you think the problem with sexual immorality in the church has diminished since Paul wrote these words? ☐ What is the basic teaching in this passage about the significance of sexual intercourse? How does this teaching differ from what is commonly held today in the secular world? ☐ What is the positive side of this teaching about our bodies? ☐ Case History: Your friend has been sexually active since he was a teenager. He has tried several times to break this habit, but failed. He now accepts the fact that he is a failure. How can you help him?

TO CLOSE/5-10 Minutes (Choose 1 or 2)

Check to see if everyone can repeat the memory verse. Encourage one another to follow through. ☐ What did you write for APPLY? ☐ What, if anything, do you feel is mastering you or almost mastering you? If this "something" is not beneficial to you, how do you think you could free yourself from it? What part would God need to play in freeing you from it? ☐ In what period of your life have you struggled with sexual temptation the most? ☐ What's the best advice you have been given on the subject of sexual temptation?

NOTES ON 1 CORINTHIANS 6:12-20

Summary ... Paul now tackles head-on the confusion that exists in the newly-formed Corinthian church over the question of sexuality. This is actually Part 2 of that discussion. In 5:1-13 he addressed a specific problem (incest). Here he discusses another problem (prostitution) and by so doing lays down some general (negative) guidelines. In chapter 7 he will discuss the positive side of sexuality when he examines marriage.

vv. 12-13 ... Paul begins with two quotations which probably reflect the views of the Corinthians. While not denying these outright, Paul does take to task the conclusions people have drawn from these maxims.

v. 12 **"Everything is permissible for me"** ... This was probably the slogan of a libertarian party at Corinth which felt that since the body was insignificant (in comparison with the "spirit") it did not really matter what one did. In one sense, this slogan is true. It defines the nature of Christian freedom and Paul does not disagree with it. He does, however, take issue with how the slogan has come to be used; i.e., as an excuse for indulgent and promiscuous behavior. He argues that while everything may be permissible, not everything is good, much less beneficial.

not everything is beneficial ... "Christian existence is dependent not upon the observance of rules, whether Jewish, pagan, gnostic,—or Christian—in origin, but solely and entirely on the free gracious activity of God, who out of pure love accepts even those who break his own laws. It does not follow, however, that it is a good and profitable thing for a Christian to exercise his freedom in an irresponsible way (cf. Galatians 5:13; also 1 Peter 2:16). In truth, only love, and actions based on love, are expedient for the people of God, since only these build up (8:1), and though obedience to law is now completely discounted as a means of justification God's law still stands (9:21), or rather has been simplified and reinforced in Christ (the law of Christ, Galatians 6:2), and may be regarded as marking out for men not a way of salvation but ways that are inexpedient, because they will lead inevitably to the collapse of society and the ruin of men's lives. Christian freedom must be limited by regard for others" (Barrett).

mastered ... To indulge one's appetites in unsuitable ways is to put oneself under the *power* of that appetite and to open the possibility of slavery to a harmful habit. So, in fact, such license is not really Christian liberty because it produces bondage!

v. 13 **"Food for the stomach ..."** ... Here also in this second slogan the low view of the gnostics towards the body asserts itself. Paul does not directly dispute this slogan either. Christians are not bound by food laws. Diet is a matter of indifference—especially in that it has no impact on one's salvation.

body ... The stomach is one thing (it will pass away in the natural course of things) but the body is something else (it will live on). "Body" means for Paul not just bones and tissues but the whole person. Sexual intercourse, unlike eating, is an act of the whole person, and therefore participates not in the transiency of material members, but in the continuity of the resurrection life" (Barrett).

not meant for sexual immorality ... Paul now qualifies his acceptance of the slogan. It appears, Barrett suggests, that the Corinthians were arguing that in the same way that it was permissible for Christians to satisfy their physical appetite without regard to law, so too they had the right to satisfy their sexual appetite with the same disregard of law. This Paul emphatically denies.

v. 14 **raise us also** ... in fact the body will be resurrected, as was the Lord's body (his was not a "spiritual" resurrection. Jesus' *body* was missing from the tomb).

v. 15 ... Since the body of the Christian belongs to the Lord and is for his use, it is inconceivable *("Never!")* that it be handed over to a prostitute.

prostitute ... Paul may not have in mind just prostitutes in general (they were numerous in a port city like Corinth) but temple prostitutes in particular. The Corinthians may have been arguing for the "right" to engage in sexually-oriented religious activities.

v. 16 **Do you not know** ... This is no new principle which Paul proposes, as he shows by quoting Genesis 2:24.

unites ... "Joined together." In its literal use this word referred to gluing things together. In its metaphorical sense here, it points to the strong bonding between two people that takes place as a result of intercourse. Intercourse is not merely an inconsequential physical act. In fact, it is akin to the bonding between the believer and the Lord, as Paul shows in verse 17 where he uses this same word.

COMMENTS

flesh ... Such uniting with a prostitute makes the two one *flesh*. This stands in contrast to becoming *one in spirit* with God (v. 17).

v. 18 **flee** ... The temptation to sexual sin was so overwhelming in Corinth that Paul uses this strong verb by way of command.

sexual immorality ... The Corinthians, not unexpectedly given the nature of life in Corinth, were confused about their sexuality. In chapter 7 it appears that many felt marriage should be avoided and certainly sexual intercourse was to be shunned between marriage partners. So here the proposition which Paul is disputing might be that since it was the duty of a husband to keep his wife "pure," if necessary he could occasionally find sexual satisfaction with a harlot (Barrett).

sins against his own body ... "My explanation is that (Paul) does not completely deny that there are other sins which also bring dishonor and disgrace upon our bodies, but that he is simply saying that these other sins do not leave anything like the same filthy stain on our bodies as fornication does" (Calvin).

v. 19 ... In 3:10 Paul pointed out that the church was the dwelling place of the Holy Spirit. Here he points to the parallel truth: so too is the individual believer.

v. 20 **bought at a price** ... The image is of ransoming slaves from their bondage. In the same way Christ paid the ransom price in order that Christians be free from the bondage of sin. Out of sheer gratitude, a Christian ought to flee sin. Out of sheer common sense, he/she should flee sin lest he/she fall back into bondage.

Prostitution in Biblical Times

Prostitution is, of course, a term which describes sexual intercourse involving people who have no binding relationship. The prostitute engages in such activity either for pay or as a form of religious activity.

The harlot who offers her body to men for a price was common in the ancient world. In first-century Israel harlots were considered in a class along with tax collectors (Matthew 21:32). In other words, they were social outcasts and were considered anathema to the Jews.

Such prostitution was condemned in the Old Testament. Warnings were given not to allow one's daughters to become harlots (Leviticus 19:29). A priest was forbidden to marry a harlot (Leviticus 21:7) and a priest's daughter who became a harlot was to be burned to death (Leviticus 21:9).

The cult prostitute was attached to a temple in which sexual activity was part of the worship process. In particular this was true of fertility cults that linked growth of the crops each spring with ritual sexual activity between devotees and representatives of the gods or goddesses.

The Old Testament also takes a strong stand against cult prostitution. For example, Deuteronomy 23:17-18 forbids Israelite men and women from becoming temple prostitutes. 2 Kings 23 describes how Israel purged itself from the Baal and Asherah which included destroying the quarters of the male shrine prostitutes (v. 7).

Old Corinth was noted for being a center of temple prostitution. A thousand prostitutes served Aphrodite, the goddess of love, whose temple sat atop the acropolis, at the base of which the city was built. The verb "to Corinthianize" *(korinthiazo)* came to mean in the ancient world "to practice fornication." New Corinth (to which Paul writes) retained the same reputation. Objects excavated from the temple in Corinth dedicated to Asclepius, the god of healing, include numerous clay models of diseased body parts. A number of these are representations of diseased sex organs, testifying to the wide spread of venereal disease.

UNIT 10—Marriage/1 Corinthians 7:1-24

TEXT

Marriage

7 Now for the matters you wrote about: It is good for a man not to marry. ²But since there is so much immorality, each man should have his own wife, and each woman her own husband. ³The husband should fulfil his marital duty to his wife, and likewise the wife to her husband. ⁴The wife's body does not belong to her alone but also to her husband. In the same way, the husband's body does not belong to him alone but also to his wife. ⁵Do not deprive each other except by mutual consent and for a time, so that you may devote yourselves to prayer. Then come together again so that Satan will not tempt you because of your lack of self-control. ⁶I say this as a concession, not as a command. ⁷I wish that all men were as I am. But each man has his own gift from God; one has this gift, another has that.

⁸Now to the unmarried and the widows I say: it is good for them to stay unmarried, as I am. ⁹But if they cannot control themselves, they should marry, for it is better to marry than to burn with passion.

¹⁰To the married I give this command (not I, but the Lord): A wife must not separate from her husband. ¹¹But if she does, she must remain unmarried or else be reconciled to her husband. And a husband must not divorce his wife.

¹²To the rest I say this (I, not the Lord): If any brother has a wife who is not a believer and she is willing to live with him, he must not divorce her. ¹³And if a woman has a husband who is not a believer and he is willing to live with her, she must not divorce him. ¹⁴For the unbelieving husband has been sanctified through his wife, and the unbelieving wife has been sanctified through her believing husband. Otherwise your children would be unclean, but as it is, they are holy.

¹⁵But if the unbeliever leaves, let him do so. A

Continued on next page

STUDY

READ

First Reading/First Impressions
Paul here strikes me as . . . ☐ anti-marriage. ☐ trying to keep the peace in mixed up marriages. ☐ trying to keep people from taking extreme actions in the name of "freedom." ☐ a real romantic (in disguise).

Second Reading/Big Idea
How would you paraphrase the key verse in this passage?

SEARCH

1. Whereas 6:12-20 dealt with sexual promiscuity, in 7:1 Paul may be quoting a faction advocating singleness and sexual abstinence even within marriage (see notes on verse 1). What reasons does Paul give for rejecting this view?

(v. 2)

(v. 3)

(v. 4)

(v. 5)

(v. 9)

2. What is the underlying principle about sex in marriage from verses 3-5?

3. Judging from verses 10-11 and 12-14, what conclusions might some of the married people have come to as a result of the notion in 7:1? How does Paul deal with these errors?

4. What principles does Paul give for Christians wondering what to do in mixed marriages where the non-believing spouse is unhappy? (vv. 15-16)

5. In light of the fact that the Corinthians were making radical, chaotic, changes in their lifestyle because of their new faith (leaving marriages, refusing to work, seeking circumcision), how would you paraphrase Paul's general rule repeated three times in verses 17, 20, and 24?

APPLY

What example can you think of where a new Christian (maybe yourself!) made some crazy changes in his or her life on the basis of their new "freedom" in Christ? What problems did that cause that applying Paul's principle could have avoided?

When is pursuing a change in circumstances appropriate?

Paul's teaching about divorce here primarily relates to the false idea that to be spiritual meant to forego sex (7:1). What principles might he suggest for a person considering divorce for other reasons (i.e., cruelty, neglect, emotional exhaustion)?

GROUP AGENDA

Divide into groups of 4 before you start to share and follow the time recommendations.

TO BEGIN/5-20 Minutes (Choose 1 or 2)

When you were younger, what married couple did you greatly admire? Why? ☐ As a young person, when you thought about marriage, what kind of person did you want to marry? How did you feel about the possibilities of remaining single? ☐ What are a couple things you learned about marriage from your parents? ☐ What did you jot down for READ in the study?

Continued on next page

believing man or woman is not bound in such circumstances; God has called us to live in peace. [16]How do you know, wife, whether you will save your husband? Or, how do you know, husband, whether you will save your wife?

[17]Nevertheless, each one should retain the place in life that the Lord assigned to him and to which God has called him. This is the rule I lay down in all the churches. [18]Was a man already circumcised when he was called? He should not become uncircumcised. Was a man uncircumcised when he was called? He should not be circumcised. [19]Circumcision is nothing and uncircumcision is nothing. Keeping God's commands is what counts. [20]Each one should remain in the situation which he was in when God called him. [21]Were you a slave when you were called? Don't let it trouble you—although if you can gain your freedom, do so. [22]For he who was a slave when he was called by the Lord is the Lord's free man; similarly, he who was a free man when he was called is Christ's slave. [23]You were bought at a price; do not become slaves of men. [24]Brothers, each man, as responsible to God, should remain in the situation God called him to.

NOTES ON 1 CORINTHIANS 7:1-24

Summary . . . Paul now addresses the concerns of married (or once married) people. In 7:25-40 he will take up the related question of whether people ought to get married. This is the fifth problem he has addressed.

v. 1 **You wrote about** . . . Up to this point Paul has been dealing with matters reported to him; but now he responds to a series of concerns about which the Corinthian Christians had written asking his advice.

to marry . . . The phrase is literally "to touch a woman" and is a common euphemism for sexual intercourse. "No where in the ancient world is this phrase used to mean 'get married' " (Fee).

It is good for a man not to marry . . . This statement probably ought to be put in quotation marks (as in 6:12-13): "It is good for a man not to touch a woman." It is quite possibly a slogan that reflects the position of an ascetic group within the Corinthian church which felt that Christian husbands who wanted to be really spiritual ought to refrain from sexual intercourse with their wives (see note on 6:18).

vv. 2-6 . . . Having quoted their position in verse 1, Paul qualifies it radically in these verses (just as he did with the slogans in 6:12).

v. 2 . . . Paul first says that it is not good for a husband and a wife to abstain from sexual relationship since this will just increase the temptation to commit adultery.

have his own wife . . . The phrase means, "to be married" or "to have sexual relations" (Fee).

vv. 3-4 . . . Paul now gives the reason for his views: There is to be complete mutuality within marriage in the matter of sexual rights. This statement stands in sharp contrast to the consensus of the first century which understood that it was the husband alone who had sexual rights and the wife simply submitted to him. For Paul, marriage is a partnership.

v. 5 . . . This is the negative form of the commandment in verses 3-4. Abstinence is allowed under two conditions: both partners agree and it is for a limited time.

deprive . . . This word could be translated "rob." For one partner to opt out of sexual relations is a form of robbery and is certainly not an act of "spirituality" as some might have been saying.

prayer . . . The purpose of such abstinence is prayer.

lack of self-control . . . Paul assumes that a couple would not be married in the first place if they did not feel any sexual desire and thus they ought to fulfill such desires legitimately lest they be tempted to adultery.

v. 6 . . . This is Paul's concession to the ascetics within the church. He modifies their maxim in verse 1 by saying, in essence, "okay, you can abstain from sexual relationships with your spouse as long as it is for a short time, by mutual consent, and that you then come back together. In any case, do not regard this as a commandment, only as a concession!"

v. 7 **were as I am** . . . i.e., celibate; though Paul is not advocating celibacy as much as resistance against inappropriate sexual expression—be this as a married or as an unmarried person.

gift . . . Paul states that celibacy is a spiritual gift! It is not a gift that everyone has. (See Unit II for the article: The Gift of Celibacy.)

vv. 8-9 . . . Paul now addresses those who were once married.

v. 8 **The unmarried and the widows** . . . The word translated *unmarried* can refer to all types of singles—bachelors, virgins, the

---

GROUP AGENDA continued

TO GO DEEPER/20 Minutes (Choose 2 or 3)

Share what you jotted down in the SEARCH portion of the Bible study. ☐ From verse 7, what do you learn of the Apostle Paul's own view of marriage? Why does he take this position? ☐ Case History: John comes home from college all excited about his new-found faith. He announces to his parents, "I'm going to drop out of school and go with a missionary to Haiti so I can preach Christ there." When you hear about this, what would you say to John?

TO CLOSE/5-20 Minutes (Choose 1 or 2)

☐ What did you write for the APPLY questions? ☐ How has singleness or marriage helped you serve Christ? ☐ How has it changed from your previous situation? ☐ By his general principle, what is Paul really saying? ("Change is usually misguided." "Think before you act." "Bloom where you are planted.") ☐ How does his principle relate to really unjust situations?

divorced, the widowed. It is also the word used ordinarily for "widowers" and it should probably be given that sense here (since otherwise why single out *widows* who are already covered in the broad term). In other words, verses 8-9 are probably directed to widowers and widows—the once married who are now unmarried due to the loss of a spouse (Fee).

it is good to stay unmarried . . . This somewhat negative view of a second marriage is consistent with Paul's view. See 7:39-40 and 1 Timothy 5:9-15.

unmarried, as I am . . . While Paul may have always been a bachelor, it is more likely that he was a widower since it was quite rare for a rabbi to be unmarried. In fact, marriage was virtually obligatory for a Jewish man.

v. 9 **cannot control themselves** . . . Literally "if they do not exercise self-control," i.e., Paul says to those formerly-married Christians who are active sexually that they ought to marry. Continence would be a particular problem for those who had once experienced an active married life but now were without a spouse.

to burn . . . When one is consumed with desire, that preoccupation makes it difficult to lead a devoted Christian life (see v. 35).

v. 10 **a wife** . . . Paul addresses his words in verses 10-11 primarily to women, probably because it was they who were advocating sexual abstinence in order to remain "spiritually pure." This may also be the reason why husbands were visiting temple prostitutes, the situation addressed in 6:12-20 (Fee).

must not separate . . . Despite his preference for the single life, Paul does *not* encourage those who are already married to be divorced.

(not I, but the Lord) . . . Paul is probably referring to statements by Jesus, as in Mark 10:2-12.

v. 11 **if she does** . . . While his prohibition against divorce is absolute, Paul does recognize that sometimes it does happen amongst Christian couples.

vv. 12-14 . . . In verses 10-11 Paul spoke to Christian couples, but here he examines the problem of marriage to a non-Christian spouse.

v. 12 **(I, not the Lord)** . . . Paul simply means that Jesus did not say anything about such mixed marriages—and so Paul cannot refer back to a saying of his (as he did in v. 10). That Jesus did not mention this is not surprising, since he ministered almost exclusively to the Jewish community and would not have been called upon to comment on marriages between Jews and Greeks.

vv. 12-13 . . . The Christian spouse is not to take the initiative to divorce his/her nonbelieving spouse if that spouse is content to remain married.

v. 14 **sanctified** . . . Not in the sense of having effected their salvation. They are, by definition, still "unbelieving" and in need of salvation (v. 16). Paul is probably arguing against the view that within mixed marriages the Christian partner is defiled. He says that, in fact, the contrary is true. "Mixed marriages are, essentially Christian marriages" (Barrett).

they are holy . . . In the Jewish community, children of Jewish parents are considered a part of the covenant and Paul probably means this sort of thing here.

v. 15 But should the non-Christian partner leave, the prohibition against divorce does not apply.

v. 16 . . . If a Christian remains in the mixed marriage, he/she may have the joy of seeing that spouse converted to Christ.

vv. 17-24 . . . Paul now gives the general principle, repeated three times (vv. 17, 20, 24), upon which he based his arguments in verses 1-16 and upon which he will also base his arguments in verses 25-40. He illustrates this principle by references to circumcision and to slavery.

v. 17 . . . Paul urges Christians to remain in whatever condition they were in when they were converted.

v. 19 . . . A Jew would dispute this hotly because to him circumcision was commanded by God. In Galatians Paul explains more thoroughly his views about circumcision.

vv. 21-23 **slave** . . . The reason why it is possible for a slave to remain content with his/her lot is because by becoming a Christian he/she will have been freed from the deeper bondage to sin, death, and the evil powers; and is, in fact, free in Christ, despite his/her social status.

UNIT 11—Virgins and Widows/1 Corinthians 7:25-40

TEXT

²⁵Now about virgins: I have no command from the Lord, but I give a judgment as one who by the Lord's mercy is trustworthy. ²⁶Because of the present crisis, I think that it is good for you to remain as you are. ²⁷Are you married? Do not seek a divorce. Are you unmarried? Do not look for a wife. ²⁸But if you do marry, you have not sinned; and if a virgin marries, she has not sinned. But those who marry will face many troubles in this life, and I want to spare you this.

²⁹What I mean, brothers, is that the time is short. From now on those who have wives should live as if they had none; ³⁰those who mourn, as if they did not; those who are happy, as if they were not; those who buy something, as if it were not theirs to keep; ³¹those who use the things of the world, as if not engrossed in them. For this world in its present form is passing away.

³²I would like you to be free from concern. An unmarried man is concerned about the Lord's affairs—how he can please the Lord. ³³But a married man is concerned about the affairs of this world—how he can please his wife—³⁴and his interests are divided. An unmarried woman or virgin is concerned about the Lord's affairs: Her aim is to be devoted to the Lord in both body and spirit. But a married woman is concerned about the affairs of this world—how she can please her husband. ³⁵I am saying this for your own good, not to restrict you, but that you may live in a right way in undivided devotion to the Lord.

³⁶If anyone thinks he is acting improperly toward the virgin he is engaged to, and if she is getting along in years and he feels he ought to marry, he should do as he wants. He is not sinning. They should get married. ³⁷But the man who has settled the matter in his own mind, who is under no compulsion but has control over his own will, and who has made up

Continued on next page

STUDY

READ

First Reading/First Impressions
My sense is that Paul . . . ☐ would never be invited to speak at a Marriage Encounter Weekend! ☐ is dealing with a situation that is irrelevant now. ☐ is trying to help the Corinthians control their sexuality.

Second Reading/Big Idea
What's the main point or topic?

SEARCH

1. In verses 25-28, how does Paul apply his general rule (7:17, 20, 24) specifically to the question of marriage and divorce? (The word for "unmarried" and "divorce" in verse 27 is the same.)

2. What does he mean by his suggestions on how to live in view of the "present crisis" in verses 29-31? (Note: Just what the "crisis" was remains unclear. It might have meant persecutions against Christians as in Acts 18:1-17, or the expected second coming of Christ.)

3. How does his advice to the married in this context (v. 29) relate to his teaching in Ephesians 5:21-33?

4. What is his point in each passage?

5. Verses 36-40 suggest that singleness is an option they ought to consider. What reasons does he give for that?

(v. 28b)

(vv. 32-34a)

(vv. 34b)

6. Whether people marry or not, how would you express his overriding concern in verse 35?

APPLY

This passage presents difficulties to the modern reader. What are some tensions you feel as you read this passage?

What possible solutions to these tensions do you see?

Whether you have never been married, are currently married, divorced, or widowed, what is one way you can show your "undivided devotion" to the Lord this week?

GROUP AGENDA

Divide into groups of 4 before you start to share and follow the time recommendations.

TO BEGIN/10 Minutes (Choose 1 or 2)

If married, tell us a bit of your "love story." How did you meet? How did you know this was "the one"? □ If not married, is that more because of your situation or a conviction? □ On a "contentment with life" scale, right now are you more like Garfield ("I hate Monday's, getting up, and work") or Odie ("Life is fun, fun, fun—let's play!")? Why? □ What did you write for READ?

TO GO DEEPER/20 Minutes (Choose 2 or 3)

Share the results of your Bible Study first—one person taking the first question, the next person the second question, etc. □ Do you feel about the present day like Paul felt about his day in verse 29? □ What is the point Paul is making in verses 32-35? Do you agree with Paul? □ Case History: Your friend's son, for whom you are like a "second parent," is

Continued on next page

---

his mind not to marry the virgin—this man also does the right thing. ³⁸So then, he who marries the virgin does right, but he who does not marry her does even better.[a]

³⁹A woman is bound to her husband as long as he lives. But if her husband dies, she is free to marry anyone she wishes, but he must belong to the Lord. ⁴⁰In my judgment, she is happier if she stays as she is—and I think that I too have the Spirit of God.

[a]*36-38 Or ³⁶If anyone thinks he is not treating his daughter properly, and if she is getting along in years, and he feels she ought to marry, he should do as he wants. He is not sinning. They should get married. ³⁷But the man who has settled the matter in his own mind, who is under no compulsion but has control over his own will, and who has made up his mind to keep the virgin unmarried—this man also does the right thing. ³⁸So then, he who gives his virgin in marriage does right, but he who does not give her in marriage does even better.*

NOTES ON 1 CORINTHIANS 7:25-40

Summary ... Having addressed married people, Paul now instructs those who are not married, focusing most of his words on women who have never been married. Here his view that the single state is preferable becomes very clear. He writes this way because he feels that Christ is about to return again. He ends this passage with a word to widows (vv. 39-40).

vv. 25-31 ... Paul makes it clear that in his view the single state is to be preferred and he gives his first reason for this: the world in its present form is passing away.

v. 25 **virgins** ... The word means those persons—either male or female—who are without sexual experience. In this passage, however, Paul uses the word to refer to women.

I give a judgment ... Paul does not have a clear word from the Lord (see note, v. 12) about whether single people ought to marry, but he does offer his own *trustworthy* opinion which he feels comes from the Lord (v. 40).

v. 26 **the present crisis** ... Paul probably has in mind the Second Coming. Since it was felt that Jesus might come again at literally any moment, everything must be put aside—including the entanglements of marriage—in order to work for God's kingdom (see v. 29).

it is good for you to remain as you are ... Again, as in 6:12, 13, 7:1, Paul appears to be quoting a truism or maxim from Corinth. But here he agrees with their slogan, though not with how they apply it, nor with the idea that it is the only perspective a Christian might have.

vv. 27-28 ... Once again Paul applies the principle found in verse 20 (and vv. 17 and 24).

v. 28 **have not sinned** ... The Corinthians have probably been insisting that unmarried men remain single. While Paul sees the wisdom of this, this is not a command (which to disobey is to sin) but simply a bit of good advice which the Christian is free to accept or reject.

many troubles ... Paul is probably thinking of the afflictions of the last days (e.g., Mark 13:7f, especially v. 17) which will only be compounded by marriage.

v. 31 **This world ... is passing away** ... The institutions of "this age" such as death, commerce, and structured relationships (like marriage) are passing away, now that Christ has ushered in the "new age." When his kingdom comes in fullness, there will be no more marriage (Mark 12:25).

vv. 32-34 ... Paul offers his second reason for preferring singleness: it enables a person to devote more energy to the service of the Lord.

v. 34 **his interests are divided** ... The married man is rightly concerned about how to please the Lord and equally right in his concern to please his wife (no less could be expected of a Christian husband). This is the problem: how to be fully faithful to both legitimate commitments.

a married woman ... The same is true of the married woman: her attention is divided in a way not true of the single woman.

v. 35 ... "The drift is clear: if you avoid marriage you avoid encumbrances, and you can devote yourself to the Lord's work without incurring problems, difficulties, and anxieties, which married people incur. But this is not rule, and indeed seemliness may be transgressed by celibacy as well as by marriage (a concession the Corinthian ascetics would probably find it very difficult to allow" (Barrett).

not to restrict you ... Literally, "not to put a halter around your neck" as one would do in order to domesticate an animal.

v. 36 **The virgin he is engaged to** ... Now Paul comes to the specific problem in Corinth. As one would expect, given the maxim in verse 26, the ascetic party is urging engaged couples to forgo marriage. While Paul would agree with this advice (since he feels that the Lord may return any day) he takes great pains to show that this is *not* the only view and that to get married is certainly not sinful. Paul is writing primarily to engaged couples; throughout this passage when he uses the word "virgin," he is probably thinking of young women engaged to be married.

GROUP AGENDA continued

considering becoming a Roman Catholic priest, but wonders about the prohibition of marriage. How do you help him sort through this issue without making up his mind for him?

TO CLOSE/5-20 Minutes (Choose 1 or 2)

What did you write for APPLY? ☐ What are your chief concerns right now? ☐ If you are married, would you agree with Paul that you cannot help but be concerned about "the affairs of this world"? ☐ What do you think God is *specifically* saying to *you* in this section of 1 Corinthians?

COMMENTS

The Gift of Celibacy

Some adult Christians are married, some are single. Obviously, more are married than are single, and this is the way God intended it to be. Many single Christian adults (not all, however) are that way because God has given them the special gift of celibacy. God has so constituted them that by remaining single they can better accomplish His will for their lives.

The gift of celibacy is the special ability that God gives to some members of the Body of Christ to remain single and enjoy it; to be unmarried and not suffer undue sexual temptation.

If you are single and know down in your heart that you would get married in an instant if a reasonable opportunity presented itself, you probably don't have the gift. If you are single and find yourself terribly frustrated by unfulfilled sexual impulses, you probably don't have the gift. But if neither of these things seems to bother you, rejoice—you may have found one of your spiritual gifts.

The biblical text for this is found in 1 Corinthians 7:7. There Paul discusses his own state of celibacy and calls it a *charisma*, a spiritual gift. Men and women who are celibate are part of God's plan for His people, and they should be accepted and honored as such.

Notice that no special gift is necessary to get married, have sexual relations, and raise a family. God has made humans with organs and glands and passions so that the majority of people, Christians included, need to get married and they do just that.

This brings up an important general principle relating to spiritual gifts: there are more members of the Body of Christ who do not share a particular spiritual gift than there are those who do. More Christians do not have the gift of celibacy than have it.

The Shakers made the mistake of universalizing the gift of celibacy, and now have all but died a natural death as a denomination. Not only did they cut off biological growth, but transfer and conversion growth became very remote possibilities for them. Their lifestyle could not appeal to very many people mainly because God has not made very many people that way.

Men and women with the gift of celibacy have tremendous advantages. Paul emphasizes these in 1 Corinthians 7. There he mentions, for example, that Christians with the gift of celibacy can actually serve the Lord better than those without it because they don't have to worry about how to please their husband or wife or family (see 1 Corinthians 7:32-34). I have found this true in my own experience. It has become more vivid since I have developed a personal friendship with John Stott, one of todays' most respected Bible teachers, authors, and Christian statesmen.

John Stott has the gift of celibacy, and because this is of special interest to me, I have observed the advantages he has over those who, like myself, do not. For one thing, I make it a habit to call home frequently when I am traveling. When I do, I usually talk to both daughters who still live at home and then to my wife, Doris. If I spend too much time traveling, I hear about it in kindly, but firm, ways. When I am home I give high priority to setting aside time to spend with my family. I plan dinner at home, Saturdays working around the house and yard with them, days out for sporting events and other entertainment, and longer camping vacations in the summer. While I am busy doing this, John Stott is writing another book or planning another conference or preparing another lecture, or traveling to another country. No wonder I can't come near to keeping up with his output. He has written so many books that some Christian bookstores now feature a special John Stott rack!

Do I envy John Stott? Not in the least. If I did, I would be untrue to what the Bible teaches about spiritual gifts. I can't thank God enough for the contribution John is making to building up Christians and to the task of world evangelization. And myself? I wouldn't trade my wife and family for a hundred special Peter Wagner racks in Christian bookstores! In fact, because I do not have the gift of celibacy, without my wife and what she contributes to every area of my being, the work I attempt to do for the Lord would be a disaster.

The temptation of gift projection is not infrequent among those with the gift of celibacy. In fact, the celibate that I am aware of who has come closest to it is the apostle Paul himself. In 1 Corinthians 7 he gets so enthusiastic about the advantages he finds in being single (the chances are he was a widower at the time, according to many biblical scholars) that he says, "I would that all men were even as myself" (1 Corinthians 7:7). But then, under the Spirit's inspiration, he catches himself and quickly says that he knows it really is a spiritual gift.—Excerpts from *Your Spiritual Gifts Can Help Your Church Grow,* by C. Peter Wagner (Glendale, CA: Regal Books) 1979, pp. 63-66.

---

v. 39 **free to marry anyone** . . . The Christian is not bound by the custom of levirate marriage whereby a brother marries the widow in order to bear a child who will carry the name of the deceased brother (Deuteronomy 25:5-10).

he must belong to the Lord . . . In fact the phrase is, literally, "only in the Lord." It is also possible to translate this phrase "remembering that *she* is a Christian." In any case, Christian widows (or widowers) may remarry but must do so in the context of their commitment to Christ.

UNIT 12—Food Sacrificed to Idols/1 Corinthians 8:1-13

TEXT

Food Sacrificed to Idols

8 Now about food sacrificed to idols. We know that we all possess knowledge.[a] Knowledge puffs up, but love builds up. ²The man who thinks he knows something does not yet know as he ought to know. ³But the man who loves God is known by God.

⁴So then, about eating food sacrificed to idols: We know that an idol is nothing at all in the world and that there is no God but one. ⁵For even if there are so-called gods, whether in heaven or on earth (as indeed there are many "gods" and many "lords"), ⁶yet for us there is but one God, the Father, from whom all things came and for whom we live; and there is but one Lord, Jesus Christ, through whom all things came and through whom we live.

⁷But not everyone knows this. Some people are still so accustomed to idols that when they eat such food they think of it as having been sacrificed to an idol, and since their conscience is weak, it is defiled. ⁸But food does not bring us near to God; we are no worse if we do not eat, and no better if we do.

⁹Be careful, however, that the exercise of your freedom does not become a stumbling block to the weak. ¹⁰For if anyone with a weak conscience sees you who have this knowledge eating in an idol's temple, won't he be emboldened to eat what has been sacrificed to idols? ¹¹So this weak brother, for whom Christ died, is destroyed by your knowledge. ¹²When you sin against your brothers in this way and wound their weak conscience, you sin against Christ. ¹³Therefore, if what I eat causes my brother to fall into sin, I will never eat meat again, so that I will not cause him to fall.

[a] *1 Or "We all possess knowledge," as you say*

STUDY

READ

First Reading/First Impressions
What song title best captures the attitude of the Corinthian church here? ☐ Love Will Find a Way ☐ I Did it My Way ☐ Praise God From Whom All Blessings Flow

Second Reading/Big Idea
If you had to choose one verse here as a slogan for a T-shirt, which would you choose? Why?

SEARCH

1. From verses 1, 4, 7 and 10 what do you imagine those on each side of the argument were saying in defense of their position? (See also COMMENTS on page 75.)

   Those saying it's OK to eat this food:

   Those saying it's not OK:

2. What "knowledge" is it that the people in verse 1 claim to have? (v. 1, also vv. 4-6)

3. Although Paul does not dispute that knowledge, what does he mean by contrasting it with love? (v. 1b)

4. What other issues does he want these people to realize are involved? (vv. 7-8, 9, 12)

5. In what way might those with "knowledge" end up really hurting others who are unsure what is right?

6. On what basis does Paul say that this issue is really irrelevant? (v. 8)

7. How is it that what is not sin for one group of people is sin for another?

8. How would you express in general terms the principle Paul applies specifically to this situation? (v. 13)

APPLY

What are some issues in your life where one person's "freedom" is another person's "stumbling block"?
- To drink or not to drink.
- To wear certain styles of clothes.
- To listen to "New Age" music or not.
- To pursue a certain standard of lifestyle.
- To be involved in certain types of groups, such as _____
- To be involved in certain political causes, such as _____
- Other _____

Of the issues where you have been on the "weak" side, how did you feel towards those who ignored your concerns?

Choose *one* of the issues where you have to deal with the question of "being a stumbling-block." Then rewrite verse 13 in your own words, applying the thought behind this verse to your particular situation. Write in the first person; i.e., "I, me. . . ."

GROUP AGENDA

Divide into groups of 4 before you start to share and follow the time recommendations.

TO BEGIN/10 Minutes (Choose 1 or 2)

☐ What was your toughest subject in school? Your easiest? ☐ Of all the knowledge you have accumulated, what subject do you know the most about? ☐ When you were a child, who was one of the most loving persons you knew? How did this person's love affect your life? ☐ What did you jot down after READ in the study?

TO GO DEEPER/20 Minutes (Choose 2 or 3)

☐ Share the results of the SEARCH portion of the Bible study first, one person sharing the first question, the next person the second questions, etc. ☐ Why do you suppose Paul begins by examining the question of "knowledge"? Who has more knowledge—the "weak brother" or the "strong"? ☐ What is the difference between being sensitive to the concerns of others, and always being controlled by other people's preferences? ☐ Case History: Your friend is an alcoholic—a "dry" alcoholic. He knows that if he takes one drink, he probably cannot stop. At the office parties, everybody takes a drink but this guy. He feels awkward. What should you do?

TO CLOSE/5-20 Minutes (Choose 1 or 2)

☐ What did you jot down for APPLY in the Bible study? ☐ Using Paul's illustration, do you look upon yourself as "weak" or "strong"? ☐ As you look back, can you remember a time when you allowed your freedom to become a stumbling block to a "weak" Christian? ☐ Where do you draw the line, or under what circumstances do you refrain from exercising your freedom? ☐ When you read verse 13, where do you need to apply this? What can you do about it this next week?

NOTES ON 1 CORINTHIANS 8:1-13

Summary ... Paul begins a rather long and somewhat convoluted section in which he ostensibly addresses the question of the Christian view of food offered to idols, but in so doing is forced to make a rather strenuous defense of his apostleship since his views on this subject of food are not at all appreciated by the Corinthians. In 8:1-13 and 10:1-13 he addresses the problem directly and in general terms. In 10:14-22 he deals with eating sacrificial food at the temples ("Don't" he says) and in 10:23—11:1 he discusses the eating of idol-food purchased in the market ("This is okay"). In chapter 9 he defends his right to be an apostle and hence to teach as he has done.

v. 1 **food sacrificed to idols** ... In ancient cities much of the food offered for sale came from the temples where it had first been offered to an idol. In fact, virtually all meat came from there since only priests were allowed by the Romans to function as butchers. Jews were absolutely forbidden to eat such idol-food and the question Paul faces here is whether the same prohibition applied to Christians.

"we all possess knowledge" ... Once again (as in 7:1) Paul appears to be quoting from their letter (see NIV footnote). As in previous instances he agrees with the assertion, but then goes on to qualify it sharply.

knowledge ... Insight into how a Christian ought to live.

knowledge puffs up ... While knowledge is useful, the basic aim of the Christian is love. Sometimes knowledge and love are even at cross purposes. When a person feels "superior" because he/she has special insights or esoteric knowledge, this attitude may make it hard to reach out in love to another person. *Knowledge* may give a person an inflated view of him/herself, while *love* is directed outward and for the benefit of the other. Love and knowledge are not mutually exclusive, though in Corinth they appeared to be.

v. 2 ... Because the Corinthians do not know that the way of love is to be preferred to the way of knowledge, they thus clearly demonstrate that they do not know as much as they think they do.

v. 3 ... Here Paul makes explicit the connection between love and knowledge. The important thing is to love God. Such love then is a clear sign that a person *is known by God* (which is more important than knowing about God).

v. 4 ... Once again Paul seems to be quoting from their letter; agreeing that idols are not truly gods because there is only one true God (He will qualify this agreement in 10:19-22). Still "Paul himself undoubtedly believed in the real existence of demonic beings, and that these beings made use of idolatrous rites; the fact that they had been defeated, and were ultimately to be completely put down, by Christ, did not remove their threat to Christians ..." (Barrett).

vv. 5-6 ... Whatever supernatural beings may exist (and in 10:19-22 Paul identifies them as demons), the fact remains that the Christian knows the one true God (he is the creator) and trusts his Son, Jesus (through whom life comes).

v. 6 **from whom all things come** ... He is the creator God.

for whom we live ... He is the one to whom our being leads; our destiny is found in him.

Lord ... In contrast to the many supposed "lords" (v. 5) stands the one true *Lord.* The title "Lord" was given to the Roman emperors, so to the Greek reader it would call attention to Jesus' divine kingship. *Lord* is also the word used frequently in the Greek Old Testament as the name of God.

Christ ... Jesus is the long-expected Jewish Messiah.

through whom ... In Jesus the creative and the redemptive work of God is seen.

v. 7 **not everyone knows this** ... The Corinthians claim to have knowledge (v. 1) yet they do not know that some Christians are not so sure that idols are without real power.

some people ... In Corinth there are those new believers who are unable to rid themselves of the sense that when they eat sacrificial food it is in honor of an idol who has real power and existence; and thus they are personally defiled by eating such food.

v. 8 **"Food does not bring us near to God"** ... Again Paul probably quotes the Corinthians and again he gives qualified approval. They are right in understanding that the observation of dietary laws has absolutely nothing to do with bringing a person to God, but they are wrong in thinking that violating such laws brings harm to no one.

COMMENTS

v. 9 **stumbling block** ... If a "strong" Christian exercises his/her right to eat idol-meat at a temple, this may induce "weak" Christians to violate their consciences, to their detriment.

weak ... Though this view is in error and really quite foolish, still Paul counsels love and consideration on the part of the "strong" (see Romans 14).

v. 10 **eating in an idol's temple** ... Now Paul comes to the real issue. The "strong" Christians were going out to dinner with friends to the local temple (these were the only "restaurants" in those days). The trouble was that the meal was part of a religious ceremony in honor of the god and, at times, ended in an orgy because cultic prostitution was an integral element of some such "worship."

v. 12 **sin against Christ** ... In fact, such offense against a weaker Christian is a *sin against Christ*. So instead of proving oneself to be "strong" and "spiritual" such a Christian is shown to have offended the law of love. Paul's whole point in chapter 8 is that Christians are meant to act on the basis of love and not to hide behind their supposed superior knowledge. It is true that idols are not true gods; that food is a matter of indifference to God; and that (by implication) Christians are free to eat what they like; but Paul's point is that such "knowledge" must be tempered by love for the weaker brother/sister who will be harmed if this knowledge is acted upon injudiciously.

Worldliness by Paul Little

I got some practical, first-hand experience with this problem at a student conference in New Jersey some years ago. There I met a fellow, a salesman, who literally worshiped baseball before he became a Christian. He would slave away all winter long so that he could be completely free for his god in the summer months. For something like twelve years he hadn't missed a single game in Philadelphia. He knew every batting average since 1910. He slept, ate, drank, and breathed baseball. Then he met the Savior and gave up his idol, leaving it at Jesus' feet.

Towards the end of our rugged and somewhat exhausting conference, this fellow overheard me suggest to another staff member, "Say, after the conference let's go over to Connie Mack Stadium and see the Phillies. They're playing the St. Louis Cards." The salesman was staggered. Incredulous, he stared at me and demanded, "How can you as a Christian go to a baseball game?" Now I've heard a lot of taboos in Christian circles, but this was the first time I'd heard baseball banned! I was flabbergasted and didn't know what to say. When he asked a second time, "How can you and Fred claim to be Christians and then go out to a ball game?" Fred and I started thinking and discussing the situation. As we talked to the salesman we uncovered his problem. Here was a man like the Gentile Christians in Rome, a former idol worshiper. Baseball had been a big thing to him; now he assumed that anybody who saw a game (ate meat), however removed from idolatrous intents, was worshiping baseball as an idol. Fred and I canceled our baseball date since our going would have needlessly disturbed our friend at a sensitive stage in his Christian life. But we also talked and counseled with him, and he gradually realized that not all Christians find baseball a problem. With his background, baseball will probably be a dangerous temptation to him for the rest of his life; this he knew. But later he also saw that he couldn't legislate for Christians who have no problem with the sport. It heartened us to see him begin to mature in his attitudes.

We have a responsibility for our weak brother. The biblical principle does not allow us to go along our way with a willy-nilly attitude, thinking "He's wrong, he's naive, he won't agree anyway, so I'll just ignore him." Nor does the biblical principle call us to conform to someone else's conscience apart from our own investigating and soul-searching. Instead, the biblical principle demands that we examine our motives: Am I doing this and not doing that because of love for Jesus Christ and a desire to honor and glorify Him? Or is the real reason a less universal one, a reason that won't hold if I move from one social or cultural group to another?...

I've found this a very helpful rule of thumb: if there is any doubt about the propriety of some activity, hold off. But if conscience is clear before God and if the thing can be done to His glory, without confusing someone else in the process, do it with pleasure. Rejoice. Be happy about whatever God has given you to enjoy. This is Paul's clear-cut principle.

Someone, of course, will always misinterpret and abuse his privilege of personal liberty by taking it as license to do whatever he pleases. Such behavior negates everything Paul is saying here. I'm always suspicious of the one who flaunts his different behavior to show how "free" he is. He's missed Paul's tone and intent by a mile.

Love is the controlling factor of all that we do when we live the whole of our lives to the glory of God. — *How to Give Away Your Faith* (Chicago: InterVarsity Press) 1966; excerpts from pp. 93-102.

UNIT 13—The Rights of an Apostle / 1 Corinthians 9:1-27

TEXT

The Rights of an Apostle

9 Am I not free? Am I not an apostle? Have I not seen Jesus our Lord? Are you not the result of my work in the Lord? ²Even though I may not be an apostle to others, surely I am to you! For you are the seal of my apostleship in the Lord.

³This is my defense to those who sit in judgment on me. ⁴Don't we have the right to food and drink? ⁵Don't we have the right to take a believing wife along with us, as do the other apostles and the Lord's brothers and Cephas?ᵃ ⁶Or is it only I and Barnabas who must work for a living?

⁷Who serves as a soldier at his own expense? Who plants a vineyard and does not eat of its grapes? Who tends a flock and does not drink of the milk? ⁸Do I say this merely from a human point of view? Doesn't the Law say the same thing? ⁹For it is written in the Law of Moses: "Do not muzzle an ox while it is treading out the grain."ᵇ Is it about oxen that God is concerned? ¹⁰Surely he says this for us, doesn't he? Yes, this was written for us, because when the plowman plows and the thresher threshes, they ought to do so in the hope of sharing in the harvest. ¹¹If we have sown spiritual seed among you, is it too much if we reap a material harvest from you? ¹²If others have this right of support from you, shouldn't we have it all the more?

But we did not use this right. On the contrary, we put up with anything rather than hinder the gospel of Christ. ¹³Don't you know that those who work in the temple get their food from the temple, and those who serve at the altar share in what is offered on the altar? ¹⁴In the same way, the Lord has commanded that those who preach the gospel should receive their living from the gospel.

¹⁵But I have not used any of these rights. And I am not writing this in the hope that you will do

Continued on next page

STUDY

READ

First Reading/First Impressions
What is your impression of what Paul is doing here? ☐ Being defensive. ☐ Answering a charge that he is not really an apostle. ☐ Illustrating what it means for him to balance love and freedom.

Second Reading/Big Idea
Which verse would you pick as the one that sums up what Paul says here?

SEARCH

1. Why do you suppose that Paul finds it necessary to interrupt his argument on eating idol-food in order to insist strenuously that he is indeed an apostle? (vv. 1-2)

2. What does the obvious answer to the four questions in verse 1 imply?

3. What three "rights" does Paul claim as an apostle? (vv. 4-6)

4. What three word pictures or metaphors does Paul use to explain his "rights"? (v. 7)

5. By citing the Old Testament example of God's concern for the ox and plowman (vv. 8-12a), and for the temple priests (vv. 13-14), what is Paul arguing for?

6. Why doesn't Paul use the "right" he has argued for? (vv. 12b, 15)

7. How is the way Paul has used his freedom in Christ (vv. 19-23) an example of the principle he called the Corinthians to follow in 8:13?

8. What is his motivation for shaping his life around the needs and concerns of others? (vv. 19, 22, 23)

9. What point is Paul making by comparing the Christian life to a race? (vv. 24-27)

APPLY

Jot down four strengths or character traits of the Apostle Paul that you find in this Scripture passage. Beside each strength, rank yourself on this strength from 1 to 10—1 being weak in this area and 10 being very strong.

PAUL'S STRENGTHS

MY SELF APPRAISAL

_____   1 2 3 4 5 6 7 8 9 10

_____   1 2 3 4 5 6 7 8 9 10

_____   1 2 3 4 5 6 7 8 9 10

_____   1 2 3 4 5 6 7 8 9 10

GROUP AGENDA

Divide into groups of 4 before you start to share and follow the time recommendations.

TO BEGIN/5-20 Minutes (Choose 1 or 2)
☐ What is one of your most vivid memories
Continued on next page

---

such things for me. I would rather die than have anyone deprive me of this boast. [16]Yet when I preach the gospel, I cannot boast, for I am compelled to preach. Woe to me if I do not preach the gospel! [17]If I preach voluntarily, I have a reward; if not voluntarily, I am simply discharging the trust committed to me. [18]What then is my reward? Just this: that in preaching the gospel I may offer it free of charge, and so not make use of my rights in preaching it.

[19]Though I am free and belong to no man, I make myself a slave to everyone, to win as many as possible. [20]To the Jews I became like a Jew, to win the Jews. To those under the law I became like one under the law (though I myself am not under the law), so as to win those under the law. [21]To those not having the law I became like one not having the law (though I am not free from God's law but am under Christ's law), so as to win those not having the law. [22]To the weak I became weak, to win the weak. I have become all things to all men so that by all possible means I might save some. [23]I do all this for the sake of the gospel, that I may share in its blessings.

[24]Do you not know that in a race all the runners run, but only one gets the prize? Run in such a way as to get the prize. [25]Everyone who competes in the games goes into strict training. They do it to get a crown that will not last; but we do it to get a crown that will last forever. [26]Therefore I do not run like a man running aimlessly; I do not fight like a man beating the air. [27]No, I beat my body and make it my slave so that after I have preached to others, I myself will not be disqualified for the prize.

[a]5 That is, Peter   [b]9 Deut. 25:4

NOTES ON 1 CORINTHIANS 9:1-27

Summary ... In proposing a serious curb on what the Corinthians have come to understand as their Christian liberty (not eating meat at the temple for the sake of their "weaker" brothers and sisters), Paul has apparently provoked a storm of opposition, especially from the libertarian party; so much so that they have begun to question his authority to write as he does. They argue in a curious way: "If Paul were really an apostle, he would certainly exercise all the rights and privileges of an apostle. But notice that he doesn't freely eat and drink; he doesn't have a wife like the other apostles; he doesn't even receive a salary from the church. He must not, therefore, be a real apostle so we don't have to listen to him."

vv. 1-2 ... Paul offers two "proofs" that he is an authentic apostle: he has seen the risen Lord and he has planted churches.

v. 1 **Am I not free?** ... In debating style, Paul disputes their accusations by asking a series of rhetorical questions. He is certainly as free as any Christian but because of his commitment to the way of love he restricts his lifestyle (as he showed in chapter 8).

Have I not seen Jesus? ... A person could not become an apostle unless he/she had witnessed first-hand the resurrected Christ (15:7-8; Acts 1:22). Since Paul had done so, he offers this as the first evidence that he is a legitimate apostle (15:3-11; Galatians 1:11-18).

The result of my work ... A true apostle will have a fruitful ministry and therefore the Corinthians are living proof of the authenticity of his ministry.

v. 2 ... While others may not consider Paul an apostle, the Corinthians certainly know better since the very existence of their church is the visible token *(seal)* of his apostleship. This is the second proof of his apostleship (2:1-5; 2 Corinthians 10:12-18).

vv. 3-6 ... Paul argues that since he is indeed an authentic apostle, he therefore has all the rights of an apostle.

v. 3 **defense** ... A technical term for the kind of defense found in a law court.

v. 4 **the right to food** ... Paul is certainly free to eat idol-food but he refuses to exercise this right because it would harm the "weaker" Christians in the community. The word "right" (or "authority") is the key word in verses 1-18.

v. 5 **the right to take a believing wife along** ... All Christians have the right to a wife (chapter 7). Additionally, apparently both the apostle and his wife were supported by the Christian community they were serving.

apostles ... Those individuals who had seen the risen Christ and who had received a commission from him. Originally the 12 but later others were so designated (Acts 14:14; Romans 16:7).

Cephas ... Peter is singled out because he had probably visited Corinth along with his wife.

v. 6 ... While apostles had the right to be supported by the church, Paul and Barnabas did not exercise this right for reasons given in verses 12f—even though the Corinthians felt that they ought to have accepted financial support (2 Corinthians 11:7-12; 12:12-13).

GROUP AGENDA continued

about being in a race (any kind of race—gunny-sack race, junior high track meet, physical education class run, etc)? ☐ What kind of work around the house do you like to do best? Least? ☐ As a kid, what was one of the toughest jobs you ever had to do? As an adult? Did you feel that the financial compensation was fair for the work involved? ☐ What did you jot down for READ?

TO GO DEEPER/20 Minutes (Choose 2 or 3)
☐ Share the results of your SEARCH in the Bible study. ☐ What is a situation where you might need to put the principle of verses 19-23 into practice? ☐ From this passage, what do you see as the obligations of a church to its pastors and leaders? ☐ Case History: Your pastor took a stand on a controversial issue which offended some of the power structure (heavy givers) in the church. They have threatened to withdraw their support if the pastor doesn't leave. What are you going to do?

TO CLOSE/5-20 Minutes (Choose 1 or 2)
☐ How did you evaluate yourself on the 4 strengths you found in Paul? ☐ In comparison to the Apostle Paul, how would you describe your own spiritual training program? ☐ When is the last time you sat down and seriously considered God's special calling for your life? What is it going to take to get you going?

vv. 7-14 ... Here Paul argues strenuously for rights which he has given up!

v. 7 **soldier** ... It would never occur to a soldier that he would be responsible to provide his own food, shelter, equipment, etc.

vineyard ... flock ... Likewise, a farmer eats his produce and a herdsman drinks his milk—even if they happen to be hired hands.

v. 8 ... Paul has just argued in verse 7 by way of analogy to common experiences. Now he argues from Scripture.

v. 9 **do not muzzle an ox** ... God commands that even an ox be allowed to eat the grain it is threshing.

v. 10 ... To the workman belongs some reward for his labor.

v. 12 **hinder the gospel** ... Were Paul to have accepted financial reward, in the Corinthian situation this might well have been misunderstood by potential converts as the major motive for his ministry.

v. 13 ... It was a widely accepted idea that those who attended to the religious needs and obligations of others were supported by those worshipers.

v. 14 ... Jesus himself indicated that converts should support their ministers (Matthew 10:10).

v. 15 **this boast** ... His "boast" is that he receives no pay as an apostle and thus there is nothing in his ministry that hinders the gospel. His second reason for taking no financial support is that this could undercut his boasting—a most surprising argument given what he has written in 1:29; 3:21; 4:7; and 5:12—though he is probably using "boast" in a "tongue-in-cheek" fashion here.

v. 16 **I cannot boast** ... Preaching is of no great credit to Paul. So compelled is he to preach that he cannot do otherwise.

v. 19 **though I am free** ... In the same way that the idea of "right" dominated verses 1-18; the idea of "freedom" is the key word in verses 19-27 (see 6:12).

I make myself a slave ... Since Paul is free he can voluntarily enslave himself to others in order that he may win them to Christ.

vv. 20-22 ... Paul is free to restrict his personal behavior for the sake of others. Thus he would not eat idol-meat when he was with Jews, legalists, or the weak. The implication is that he could (and probably did) eat idol-meat with Gentiles (though not at temples).

v. 20 **I became like a Jew** ... Paul was, of course, a Jew by birth, but as a result of his conversion he was freed from the law and its obligations; yet in order to win other Jews, in certain instances he behaved as if he were back under law—though understanding all the time that this was not the means by which he came to know God.

v. 21 ... Likewise, in other instances he behaves as if he were outside all law. Yet so as not to leave the Corinthians with the impression that a Christian could do whatever he/she wanted without regard to its morality, he also points to *Christ's law* (the law of love) to which he is obedient.

v. 22 **the weak** ... Those with weak consciences (see 8:7-13) who are not yet free from legalism or from the power of paganism. Paul voluntarily abstained from that which offended the weak.

save some ... The real issue is salvation, not just persuading people to join the church.

vv. 24-27 ... Paul turns to the concept of self-discipline by way of transition to chapter 10. Discipline was exactly what the Corinthians had most need of.

v. 24 ... "The weight of his argument is directed simply against the notion that there is an automatic connection between running and winning. There is none. The Christian must not only start but continue in the right way; it is implied that he must put forth all his strength. The process also implies self-discipline—not a strong point with the Corinthians" (Barrett).

v. 25 **crown** ... In the Greek games the winner received a crown made of pine boughs. The Christian's crown is eternal life.

vv. 26-27 ... The body is not an enemy. It is simply that it responds readily to temptation and must be disciplined to be of service to God.

UNIT 14—Warnings from Israel's History / 1 Corinthians 10:1-13

TEXT

Warnings from Israel's History

10 For I do not want you to be ignorant of the fact, brothers, that our forefathers were all under the cloud and that they all passed through the sea. ²They were all baptized into Moses in the cloud and in the sea. ³They all ate the same spiritual food ⁴and drank the same spiritual drink; for they drank from the spiritual rock that accompanied them, and that rock was Christ. ⁵Nevertheless, God was not pleased with most of them; their bodies were scattered over the desert.

⁶Now these things occurred as examples,[a] to keep us from setting our hearts on evil things as they did. ⁷Do not be idolaters, as some of them were; as it is written: "The people sat down to eat and drink and got up to indulge in pagan revelry."[b] ⁸We should not commit sexual immorality, as some of them did—and in one day twenty-three thousand of them died. ⁹We should not test the Lord, as some of them did—and were killed by snakes. ¹⁰And do not grumble, as some of them did—and were killed by the destroying angel.

¹¹These things happened to them as examples and were written down as warnings for us, on whom the fulfillment of the ages has come. ¹²So, if you think you are standing firm, be careful that you don't fall! ¹³No temptation has seized you except what is common to man. And God is faithful; he will not let you be tempted beyond what you can bear. But when you are tempted, he will also provide a way out so that you can stand up under it.

[a] 6 Or *types*; also in verse 11   [b] 7 Exodus 32:6

STUDY

READ

First Reading/First Impressions
What saying best catches the idea here? ☐ Those who fail to learn from history are doomed to repeat it. ☐ Just because you were born in a garage doesn't make you a car. ☐ Pride cometh before a fall.

Second Reading/Big Idea
What's the main point or topic?

SEARCH

1. What does Paul's reminder to them of the discipline needed to "run the race" (9:24-27), and this example of Israel's past (10:1-5) show about some of the attitudes in the Corinthian church?

2. What five things does Paul cite that showed the privileged position of the children of Israel? (vv. 1-4)

3. What point is Paul making in showing that these "sacraments" failed to protect Israel from God's anger?

4. What attitude is he exposing in this history lesson? (v. 6)

64

5. What four problems in the church at Corinth are warned against? (vv. 7-10) What happened to the children of Israel when they engaged in these activities?

6. Why does Paul warn the Corinthians in particular? (v. 11)

7. How does Paul's example of the racer (9:24-25) illustrate what he means by "being careful"? (v. 12)

8. What are four principles or statements Paul makes about temptation? (v. 13)

APPLY

Here is another one of those promises in the Scripture that you should commit to memory if you have not already. Photocopy the verse or write it out on a 3 × 5 card and place it on the dashboard or over the kitchen sink for constant reference. See if you can commit to memory this verse before your next group meeting.

"No temptation has seized you except what is common to man. And God is faithful; he will not let you be tempted beyond what you can bear. But when you are tempted, he will also provide a way out so that you can stand up under it."
1 Corinthians 10:13 NIV

GROUP AGENDA

Divide into groups of 4 before you start to share and follow the time recommendations.

TO BEGIN/10 Minutes (Choose 1 or 2)

☐ What are two things you remember about your grandfather? ☐ Who is the big "storyteller" in your family—who keeps alive the stories of your family heritage? ☐ What did you jot down under READ?

TO GO DEEPER/20 Minutes (Choose 2 or 3)

☐ Share the SEARCH portion of the Bible study, one person answering the first question, the next person the second question, etc. ☐ To what events in Israel's history is Paul referring in verses 1-5? (See Exodus 13-17) In what way are these events parallel to events in a Christian's journey today? ☐ What is the spiritual principle or lesson you get from this passage? What is the warning? What is the great promise? ☐ Case History: Your roommate grew up in a strong Christian home, went to a great church, and committed himself to Christ early in life. But something happened when he went away to college. He forgot about his spiritual roots, made fun of his "old fashioned" church, and delighted in "pushing the limits" against God. Last night, he asked if you minded if he brought his girlfriend to the room for the weekend. What do you say?

TO CLOSE/5-20 Minutes (Choose 1 or 2)

☐ Check to see if everyone can repeat the Scripture verse word perfect. Encourage one another in this project. ☐ What kind of spiritual heritage did your forefathers leave you? What would you like to pass on to your kids? ☐ From your own experience, could you verify the promise in verse 13? How? ☐ What is one of the struggles you are dealing with now? What does God say to you about this struggle from verse 13?

NOTES ON 1 CORINTHIANS 10:1-13

Summary ... Paul now returns to his main theme (sacrificial food) from which he digressed in Chapter 9 in order to defend his apostleship. He reasserts this theme by expanding on the idea of self-discipline with which he concluded chapter 9 (vv. 24-27). "The Corinthians took an easy view of sacrificial food (a view that was not the same as what Paul understood by Christian freedom) because they did not take idolatry seriously; and they did not take idolatry seriously (so the present paragraph suggests) because they believed that the Christian rites of Baptism and the Supper secured them from any possible harm. This was a mistake which Paul, who had just acknowledged (9:27) the peril in which he himself stood, exposed by the use of Old Testament analogies" (Barrett).

v. 1 **ignorant** ... Though they claimed to have "knowledge" (8:1-2), in fact they had really misunderstood the meaning of baptism and communion.

our forefathers ... Though his leaders are largely Gentiles, Paul considers them the spiritual heirs of Israel.

cloud/sea ... Paul reminds them of the Exodus (Exodus 13:21; 14:19-31).

vv. 2-4 ... Paul notes that the Israelites had experiences which parallel the basic Christian rites: the passage through the Red Sea is analogous to baptism; the manna they ate (Exodus 16:4, 13-18) and the water they drank (Exodus 17:6; Numbers 20:6-13) were analogous to the bread and wine in communion.

vv. 3-4 **spiritual food/drink** ... Not only did these gifts from God nourish their physical bodies, they had an additional spiritual function in that they were symbols which prefigured Christian communion and hence the benefits of Christ's death.

v. 4 **that rock was Christ** ... The spiritual benefits for the Israelites derived from this supernaturally-provided water accrued from Christ's still-to-come work.

v. 5 **Nevertheless** ... Even though God had supplied the Israelites with analogous sacraments by which they benefited from Christ, this alone was not enough. The Israelites still sinned and thus were denied entrance into the promised land, dying instead in the desert.

vv. 6-10 ... "Some Corinthians believed that their participation in the Christian sacraments guaranteed them against any possible loss of future salvation. They might commit idolatry (v. 7) and fornication (v. 8), they might tempt God (v. 9) and complain against him (v. 10) with impunity because they had been baptized and received the eucharist. Paul admits to no such ... sacramental efficacy ..." (Barrett).

v. 6 **examples** ... In the same way, "if God did not spare them, he will not spare us, for our situation is the same as theirs" (Calvin).

on evil things as they did ... Numbers 11:4-34.

v. 7 ... Paul is warning against participation in pagan temple worship (see note 8:10).

v. 8 **sexual immorality** ... Paul now explicitly condemns the sexual vice associated with pagan religion (6:12-20).

twenty-three thousand ... Paul is referring to the story of the Israelites' fornication with the Moabite women as recorded in Numbers 25:1-9 (the figure there is 24,000). Paul's estimate is either due to a lapse of memory or it is an error in the text which crept in at a later stage when this letter was being copied by a scribe. "Paul rarely quotes scripture with verbatim accuracy; no one did in those days. There was no such thing as a concordance to help find a passage easily; scripture was not written in books because books had not yet been invented but on wieldy rolls" (Barclay).

v. 9 **test the Lord** ... The Corinthians (as had the Israelites before them) were testing God by these actions; they were seeing how much they could get away with (10:22).

killed by snakes ... See Numbers 21:4-9 and Psalms 78:18.

v. 10 **grumble** ... They were also grumbling against Paul for telling them not to engage in temple feasts and ritual prostitution.

The destroying angel ... it is not clear what Paul is referring to here. Certainly there is ample evidence of grumbling (Numbers 14-17) but these passages do not mention an avenging angel, though "the passages mentioned ... were taken by the Rabbis as evidence for the existence of a special destroying angel, and Paul's noun with the definite article, suggests that he shared this belief" (Barrett).

COMMENTS

v. 11 ... The Corinthians, in their pride and arrogance, were misunderstanding the very foundation of their faith. Trusting the sacraments and not Christ, they were headed for a rude awakening if they failed to heed these warnings.

v. 12 ... Israel felt it was secure (they could point to God's special provisions for them which were prototypes of the Christian sacraments) yet they lapsed into sin and experienced the resultant destruction. So too the Corinthians were headed for the same fate regardless of the sacrament.

v. 13 ... Paul encourages the Corinthians to stand firm by reminding them that when Christians resist sin they do so in the knowledge that they will be able to endure.

temptation ... Paul has identified various temptations which Israel faced: the temptation to idolatry, the temptation to commit sexual immorality, the temptation to test God, and the temptation to grumble about where God led them. To be tempted is to be tested. Facing the choice of deserting God's will or doing God's will, the person must either resist or yield. Temptation is not sin. Yielding is. The Corinthians do not have to give in to the strong pull of their pagan past nor do they have to indulge their appetites without restraint.

a way out ... Temptation, it seems, is not unusual nor unexpected. Resisting it is not pleasant but the Christian can do so. There will be *a way out* for those who seek it. The Greek word here is *ekbasis* and was used to describe a narrow pass through the mountains.

Temptation

by John White

Have you ever fooled around with a piano? Open the top. Press the loud pedal. Then sing a note into the piano as loudly as you can. Stop and listen. You will hear at least one cord vibrating in response to the note you sang. You sing—and a string in the piano picks up your voice and plays it back.

Here, then, is a picture of temptation. Satan calls and you vibrate. The vibration is the "lust" James speaks of. Your desire is to go on responding to his call. If pianos have feelings, I imagine they are "turned on" when the cord vibrates. There is nothing bad about vibrating. The cord was made to vibrate and to vibrate powerfully. But it was meant to vibrate in response to a hammer—not in response to a voice.

The appropriate response, then, is not to vibrate rapturously to the voice of the devil but to release the loud pedal and close the top of the piano. As Luther put it quaintly, you cannot stop birds flying about your head, but you can prevent them from building a nest in your hair.

In more concrete terms, whether vibration consists of sexual arousal, angry feelings, a desire to possess something beautiful or whatever, the vibration itself is not evil. Sexual arousal has its place. The question is under what circumstances? Or again, is this the appropriate object and this the appropriate occasion? If not, slam down the lid of the piano and get your big foot off the loud pedal!

While there exists an infinite variety of notes the devil can whistle, his temptations fall under three broad groupings: the lust of the flesh, the lust of the eye and the pride of life....

Yet we should not concern ourselves with the form of temptation but with how to resist it. Let me be very simple. Satan tempts from behind. "Look," he whispers, "Isn't it beautiful? Just think what you could do ... what people would say ... how you would be admired ... how much power you would have ... look, look, LOOK!" The Bible gives us two complementary counsels about temptation, one on temptation itself and the other on the tempter. Concerning temptation we are simply told: Flee temptation. Concerning the tempter the word is: Resist the devil and he will flee from you.

Think how these two counsels work together. Did you ever run away from something and face it at the same time? How could you?

Never face temptation. Flee from it. And in fleeing, turn your back on it. And in turning, whom will you face? Who has been standing behind you and whispering vivid word-pictures in your ear? Turn and face him. Resist him. And his Satanic Majesty will withdraw.

Many commentators have pointed out that when Jesus was tempted in the wilderness he responded to each satanic suggestion with the words, "it is written ... it is written ... it is written." Each time that Jesus employed the sword of the Spirit, he slashed the tempter.

Many Christians have testified to the astonishing effect particular Scriptures have in their ability to cope with temptation. The Bible is called the sword of the Spirit for three reasons: The Spirit inspired it; the Spirit will place it in your hands and teach you skill in using it; the Spirit will make it cut deep. Therefore get to know Scripture. And as you turn your back on temptation and face your Tempter, reach out your hand for the sword which the Spirit will place in your grasp. Then plunge it deep into the Tempter and hear him howl in pain as he flees back to hell.—from *The Fight* (Downers Grove, Ill.: InterVarsity Press, 1976) excerpts from pp. 78-82.

UNIT 15—Idol Feasts and the Lord's Supper / 1 Cor. 10:14-22

TEXT

Idol Feasts and the Lord's Supper

¹⁴Therefore, my dear friends, flee from idolatry. ¹⁵I speak to sensible people; judge for yourselves what I say. ¹⁶Is not the cup of thanksgiving for which we give thanks a participation in the blood of Christ? And is not the bread that we break a participation in the body of Christ? ¹⁷Because there is one loaf, we, who are many, are one body, for we all partake of the one loaf.

¹⁸Consider the people of Israel: Do not those who eat the sacrifices participate in the altar? ¹⁹Do I mean then that a sacrifice offered to an idol is anything, or that an idol is anything? ²⁰No, but the sacrifices of pagans are offered to demons, not to God, and I do not want you to be participants with demons. ²¹You cannot drink the cup of the Lord and the cup of demons too; you cannot have a part in both the Lord's table and the table of demons. ²²Are we trying to arouse the Lord's jealousy? Are we stronger than he?

STUDY

READ

First Reading/First Impressions
What tone do you "hear" in this passage? ☐ Like a friend to friend talk. ☐ Like a parent pleading with a child to behave. ☐ Like a teacher instructing a class. ☐ _____

Second Reading/Big Idea
In a sentence, what is Paul's main concern here?

SEARCH

1. What is Paul's simple command when it comes to whether or not believers should eat the meals involved with pagan temples? (v. 14)

2. His first support for his call to avoid these meals appeals to the nature of the Lord's Supper. How would you explain to a friend what he means by saying that drinking the cup and eating the bread is a "participation" in Christ's blood and body? (Other relevant Scripture includes Luke 22:19-20, John 6:53-57.)

3. His second support comes from Israel's experience with sacrificial meals (v. 18). What is his point in mentioning that those who ate of the sacrifices actively participated in the meaning of that sacrifice?

4. How does the fact that eating the Lord's Supper is a "participation" in Christ just as eating the Jewish sacrifices was a "participation" in the meaning of that sacrifice relate to his call to avoid participation in the feasts at pagan temples? (vv. 14, 20)

5. Although he has dismissed the reality of idols as such in 8:4, from 8:10 and 10:20, what is the real danger related being involved in the activities at pagan temples?

6. What teaching about the Lord's Supper does Paul give in chapter 10?

WHERE DID THE LORD'S SUPPER HAVE ITS ORIGIN? (vv. 3-4)

WHAT DOES THE CUP REPRESENT? (v. 16)

WHAT DOES THE BREAD REPRESENT? (v. 16)

WHAT DOES THE LORD'S SUPPER CREATE? (v. 17)

APPLY

Idolotry can take many forms. List one or two "idols" which you see being worshipped in contemporary society.

Examine you own life. What is one potential "idol" you have to guard against?

What is God saying to you about this "idol" in verse 14?

GROUP AGENDA

Divide into groups of 4 before you start to share and follow the time recommendations.

TO BEGIN/10 Minutes (Choose 1 or 2)

☐ What are two things you're really thankful for this week? ☐ How did the crowd you ran around with in junior high influence you? ☐ What was one of the best parties you ever attended? Why was it so good? ☐ What did you jot down in the Bible Study under READ?

TO GO DEEPER/20 Minutes (Choose 2 or 3)

☐ Share the SEARCH portion of your Bible study. ☐ What is the spiritual lesson or principle concerning "idol feasts" and how would this principle apply to our culture today? ☐ Why is the experience of going to a feast and eating meat and drinking wine offered to idols more serious than buying the same meat after it was offered and eating it at home? (1 Corinthians 8). ☐ What is Paul really saying in verse 22? See James 4:4-6.
☐ Case History: Mary is a Christian. She also likes to follow the horoscope, play with ouija boards and tarot cards and occasionaly go to a party where they try to communicate with dead "spirits"--just for fun. Recently she talked about her freedom in the Bible study group. How would you handle her?

TO CLOSE/5-20 Minutes (Choose 1 or 2)

☐ What did you jot down for APPLY in the Bible study? ☐ How does it make you feel when you spend a lot of time with people who are "worshiping" objects other than God? ☐ When, if ever, have you played around with ouija boards, tarot cards, etc.? Do you feel this is participating with demons? Why? ☐ What do you believe about Satan and demons? How do you keep yourself free from being influenced by these powers?

NOTES ON 1 CORINTHIANS 10:14-22

Summary . . . Paul now directly prohibits attendance at idol feasts because he understands such sacred meals to involve actual fellowship with the demonic. It is clear from his survey of the history of Israel (vv. 1-13) that being one of God's chosen people is no automatic guarantee that one will not fall into idol worship. The pursuit of false gods was a constant temptation to Israel. Likewise Christians must not lapse into idol worship.

v. 14 **Therefore** . . . Paul will now draw the logical conclusions from his survey of Israel's past.

my dear friends . . . They may ignore Paul. They may chafe at his authority. They may refuse his advice, but still they are all bound deeply together. Paul is not addressing strangers but the very people he introduced to Christ in the first place.

flee from idolatry . . . In the same way that he unequivocally forbids fornication (6:18) so too he forbids Christians from participating in idol worship. Neither fornication nor idol feasts is an option for the Christian. While Paul does counsel Christians to "stand fast" in the face of evil (Ephesians 6:10-18), when it comes to "sins of the flesh" he counsels flight—not a fight. The temptations are simply too strong to resist. The Corinthians are to stay away from the pagan temples.

v. 15 . . . Paul appeals to the fact that the Corinthians consider themselves to be wise people. It is a matter of common sense, which surely they recognize, that the worship of idols is the opposite of the worship of God.

sensible people . . . This is said with some irony. They may think themselves "sensible," but up to this point, they have not demonstrated it.

v. 16 **The cup of thanksgiving** . . . This was the cup of wine drunk at the conclusion of the meal in a Jewish home over which a blessing was spoken: "Blessed art thou, O Lord, our God, who givest us the fruit of the vine." In the Passover meal this was the third of four cups of wine. During the Last Supper, Jesus made this cup a symbol of his soon-to-be-shed blood, to be drunk therefore in remembrance of him.

participation . . . By drinking the wine and eating the bread, Christians have actual fellowship with Christ. They enjoy together the benefits his death secured for them.

v. 17 . . . Furthermore, sharing together the one loaf is a demonstration of the fact that all Christians are unified in one body. Such unity should express itself in love for one another. This is another argument for not trampling on the sensibilities of one's "weaker brother."

v. 18 **eat the sacrifices** . . . The priests were allowed to eat parts of the sacrificial offerings (Leviticus 10:12-15) as were others in certain instances (1 Samuel 9:10-24).

participate in the altar . . . Those who offered sacrifices shared in both the physical and the spiritual benefits of the sacrifice. The basic idea is that those who share in an act also share in the meaning and benefits of that act.

v. 19 . . . In and of itself, the food offered to an idol is not changed by that act. This is why Paul allows Christians to purchase such meat from the market (v. 25) and to eat it at the home of unbelieving friends (v. 27).

v. 20 **But** . . . Although food is not contaminated *per se* by being offered to an idol, when it is eaten at a temple in the context of idol worship it becomes evil because it demeans God and robs him of worship rightfully his (Romans 1:22-25). It also brings even unwitting "guests" into contact with evil powers. "At such a feast it was always held that the god himself was a guest. Moreover, it was often held that after the meat had been sacrificed the god himself was in it and that at the banquet he entered into the very bodies and spirits of those who ate. Just as an unbreakable bond was forged between two men if they ate each other's bread and salt, so a sacrificial meal formed a real communion between the god and his worshipers" (Barclay).

demons . . . Paul knew that the stone idol was just a stone; but he also knew that it was the dwelling place of authentic, evil supernatural beings with which it was dangerous to come into contact (See Deuteronomy 32:16-17; Psalm 106:36-39).

participants . . . Or "partners with demons." The danger in eating at a temple is in developing relationships with the demonic.

v. 21 . . . Paul is unequivocal. A Christian cannot participate in both the Lord's Supper and in a demon feast at a temple.

COMMENTS

Demons

The issue, as it turns out, is not so much idols as it is demons. Idols are literally "images." They are images—cast in wood, stone, paint, etc., which depict a god and which are the objects of worship. These, Paul says, mean nothing. They are dumb stone and dead wood.

But demons are another matter. Demons are a distinct order of spiritual being hostile to God and to human beings. They are most real and bent on our harm and destruction. In the New Testament we read about demons possessing people (e.g., Mark 5:1-20) and about them causing a variety of maladies including dumbness (Luke 11:14) and epilepsy (Mark 9:14-29). Some of the demons are named: Belial, Beelzebub, and, of course, Satan. In the New Testament, Jesus is shown to have great power over demons. By casting out demons he demonstrates the nature of his kingdom. It will be by the works of Jesus that the power of Satan is overcome and undone. Jesus gave to his disciples the same power to cast out demons (Luke 9:1).

This New Testament belief in the reality of demons was widely shared:

> The Jews, and indeed the whole ancient world, believed strongly in demons and devils. As Harnack put it, "The whole world and the circumambient atmosphere were filled with devils; not merely idolatry, but every phase and form of life was ruled by them. They sat on thrones, they hovered around cradles. The earth was literally a hell."
>
> Dr. A. Rendle Short cites a fact which shows the intensity with which the ancient world believed in demons. In many ancient cemeteries skulls were found which had been trepanned. That is to say, a hole had been bored in the skull. In one cemetery, out of one hundred twenty skulls, six had been trepanned. With the limited surgical technique available that was no small operation. Further, it was clear from the bone growth that the trepanning had been done during life. It was also clear that the hole in the skull was too small to be of any physical or surgical value; and it is known that the removed disc of bone was often worn as an amulet round the neck. The reason for the trepanning was to allow the demon to escape from the body of the man. If primitive surgeons were prepared to undertake that operation, and if men were prepared to undergo it, the belief in demon-possession must have been intensely real.
>
> The collective word for demons is *mazzikin,* which means one who does harm. So the demons were malignant beings intermediate between God and man who were out to work men harm.
>
> The demons, according to Jewish belief, could eat and drink and beget children. They were terrifyingly numerous. There were, according to some, seven and a half millions of them; every man had ten thousand on his right hand and ten thousand on his left. They lived in unclean places, such as tombs and spots where there was no cleansing water. They lived in the desert where their howling could be heard—hence the phrase "a howling desert." They were specially dangerous to the lonely traveller, to the woman in child-birth, to the bride and bridegroom, to children who were out after dark, and to those who voyaged at night. They were specially active in the midday heat and between sunset and sunrise. There was a demon of blindness and a demon of leprosy and a demon of heart-disease. They could transfer their malign gifts to men. For instance, the evil eye which could turn good fortune into bad and in which all believed was given to a man by the demons. They worked along with certain animals—the serpent, the bull, the donkey and the mosquito. The male demons were known as *shedim,* and the female as *lilin,* after Lilith. The female demons had long hair and were the enemies of children. That is why children had their guardian angels (Matthew 18:10)....
>
> There were many exorcists who claimed to be able to cast out demons. So real was this belief that by A.D. 340 the Christian church actually possessed an Order of Exorcists. But there was this difference—the ordinary Jewish and pagan exorcist used elaborate incantations and spells and magical rites. Jesus with one word of clear, simple, brief authority exorcised the demon from a man. No one had ever seen anything like this before. The power was not in the spell, the formula, the incantation, the elaborate rite; the power was in Jesus and men were astonished.
>
> What are we to say to all this? Paul Tournier in *A Doctor's Casebook* writes, "Doubtless there are many doctors who in their struggle against disease have had, like me, the feeling that they were confronting, not something passive, but a clever and resourceful enemy." Dr. Rendle Short comes tentatively to the conclusion that "the happenings in this world, in fact, and its moral disasters, its wars and wickedness, its physical catastrophies, and its sicknesses, may be part of a great warfare due to the interplay of forces such as we see in the book of *Job,* the malice of the devil on one hand and the restraints imposed by God on the other." *(The Gospel of Mark* by William Barclay [Philadelphia: The Westminster Press, 1975] pp. 33-36.)

Thus Paul tells the Corinthians to "Flee from idolatry." The idols may be nothing, but there is an evil power behind them which can possess. To come in contact with demons is to lay oneself open to evil. Thus it is quite clear that Christians are not to be "participants with demons" in any way.

UNIT 16—The Believer's Freedom/1 Corinthians 10:23-11:1

TEXT

The Believer's Freedom

23"Everything is permissible"—but not everything is beneficial. "Everything is permissible"—but not everything is constructive. 24Nobody should seek his own good, but the good of others.

25Eat anything sold in the meat market without raising questions of conscience, 26for, "The earth is the Lord's, and everything in it."

27If some unbeliever invites you to a meal and you want to go, eat whatever is put before you without raising questions of conscience. 28But if anyone says to you, "This has been offered in sacrifice," then do not eat it, both for the sake of the man who told you and for conscience' sake—29the other man's conscience, I mean, not yours. For why should my freedom be judged by another's conscience? 30If I take part in the meal with thankfulness, why am I denounced because of something I thank God for?

31So whether you eat or drink or whatever you do, do it all for the glory of God. 32Do not cause anyone to stumble, whether Jews, Greeks or the church of God—33even as I try to please everybody in every way. For I am not seeking my own good but the good of many, so that they may be saved. 11 1Follow my example, as I follow the example of Christ.

[a]26 Psalm 24:1   [b]28 Some manuscripts conscience' sake, for *"the earth is the Lord's* and everything in it"

STUDY

READ

First Reading/First Impressions
How would you feel as a Corinthian after all Paul has said about this food issue? ☐ I guess it's a matter of who's around. ☐ But I like those feasts! ☐ I'm confused: first he says it's OK, then it's not, then it is.

Second Reading/Big Idea
Paraphrase what you see as the key verse in this section.

SEARCH

1. Compare verse 23 with 6:12. How is Paul's argument here about participating in the idol's feasts similar to his approach to the matter of sexual immorality?

2. Compare verse 24 with 8:1b, and 13. From these passages, how would you explain the way a Christian is to use his or her freedom?

3. Getting back to the issue of whether or not to eat the sacrificial meat sold in the public meat markets, what is Paul's counsel? (vv. 25, 27) How does he justify it? (v. 26)

4. Even in private, when is it proper to abstain from eating this meat? (vv. 28-29)

5. Who is the "anyone" in verse 28? ☐ The non-believer who invites you to dinner. ☐ Another Christian guest who has qualms about eating the meat. How can you support your answer?

6. In summary, what makes it all right normally to eat this sacrificial meat in private, but not at the temple feasts? (See also 8:4, 7, 10; 10:14, 20-21)

7. What are the basic principles Paul gives for making decisions in these unclear areas?

(10:31)

(10:32)

(10:33)

(11:1)

APPLY

When it comes to making "judgment calls" in grey areas, what are three guidelines (given in verses 31-33) you should consider? Try to restate these guidelines in the form of questions.

Can you apply these guidelines to a "grey area" situation in which you currently find yourself?

GROUP AGENDA

Divide into groups of 4 before you start to share. And follow the time recommendations.

TO BEGIN/10 Minutes (Choose 1 or 2)

☐ What is one of the worst experiences you ever had with food? One of the best? ☐ What was one of the nicest things somebody did for you this week? One of the nicest things you did for somebody else? ☐ If you won a contest which entitled you to take as much as you could from a gourmet food shop for 5 minutes, what would you go for? (List the top five items) ☐ What did you jot down in your Bible study under READ?

TO GO DEEPER/20 Minutes (Choose 2 or 3)

☐ Share the results of your SEARCH in the Bible study—one person sharing question 1, the next person question 2, etc. ☐ What is the difference between going to a feast where idol-meat is served (10:14-22) and going to a meat market and buying the same meat? What's the lesson or principle here? ☐ Why are you allowed to eat meat with an unbeliever, but told not to eat meat if someone reminds you that it was offered as an idol sacrifice? What makes the same act okay in one instance and wrong in another instance? ☐ Case History: On a tour of the Holy Land with your pastor you were introduced to wine for the first time. Your pastor graciously went along with the custom in Israel and drank, and so did you. On your return, you invite over friends to see your slides. Should you take out the slides which show your group drinking wine?

TO CLOSE/5-20 Minutes (Choose 1 or 2)

☐ What did you put down for questions on making "judgment calls"? ☐ What "grey issues" are you struggling with at the moment? In business? ☐ How well does your life reflect "doing all for the glory of God"?

NOTES ON 1 CORINTHIANS 10:23-11:1

Summary ... Paul now sums up the discussion he began in 8:1 concerning food offered to idols by setting out specific, practical instructions.

v. 23 ... Paul begins by quoting for a second time a popular maxim in the Corinthian Church. In 6:12 he examined the implications of this for an individual Christian, warning that unrestrained personal freedom can lead to a form of bondage. Here he examines the implications of this maxim *for the church as a whole,* arguing that not all activities build up the body. "The freedom of the Christian is the freedom to play his part in the upbuilding of the community" (Barth).

v. 24 ... This is the maxim that ought to guide their behavior.

others ... Christians ought to seek good, not just for their friends, but even for those who are unlike them. Here, specifically, Paul is urging consideration for those who disagree about eating idol-food.

v. 25 ... It does not matter what one eats—food offered to idols or food prohibited by strict Jewish dietary laws. Neither abstinence nor partaking has any effect on one's relationship to God.

v. 26 ... All food is a gift from God.

v. 27 ... Paul shifts his focus from food purchased by a Christian in the market for use at his/her own home to the related question of what one might eat or not eat at the home of a non-Christian friend. In this case, the Christian can eat whatever is placed before him/her, although here the scruples of one's dinner companions must also be considered.

v. 28 **anyone** ... It is probably a pagan who points out that what is being offered is idol-food, knowing his fellow guest to be a Christian, and knowing that Jews were hypersensitive about what they ate (to the pagan, Christianity was merely a Jewish sect). The warning is probably offered out of a sense of concern (Fee).

offered in sacrifice ... To this point in the text Paul has consistently used the word *eidolothata* to describe such food. This was a word used in a negative, belittling sense by those who opposed idolatry. The term here, *hierothuta*, is the word used by pagans themselves to describe what they understood to be sacred food.

v. 29b **For why should my freedom be judged by another's conscience?** ... This is Paul's basic point: Christians can eat idol-food freely in homes because they are the Lord's and are not enslaved to anyone else.

v. 30 ... As in verse 26 Paul points out that even "idol-food" comes from God and is a source of thanksgiving.

v. 31 ... This is a positive restating of what has been put negatively in verses 25-30. Use eating and drinking to bring glory to God; not to cause strife nor to honor a demon.

v. 32 ... Paul restates what he has said in 8:13; 9:19-23; and 10:23-24. In fact the word translated "to stumble" probably ought to be translated "to offend;" i.e., Paul says, "try to live without 'offending' in any direction" (Fee).

v. 33 **I try to please everybody** ... This is Paul's aim, though the hostility of the Corinthians themselves show that he did not always succeed.

not seeking my own good ... Paul explains what he means. It is not merely a matter of ingratiating oneself with others in order to gain favor or avoid hardship. (This he condemns in Galatians 1:10.) Rather, his motive is to create openness to the gospel so that men and women will come to faith.

11:1 **follow my example** ... As an apostle, it was not just his responsibility to teach and preach the gospel but to live it out in such a way that people would see for themselves what it meant to be a Christian. When establishing new churches, Paul might have been the *only* Christian the new converts had met and thus their only model.

the example of Christ ... For his part, he bases his life on the example of Jesus.

COMMENTS

The Weak and the Strong

Who are the people to whom Paul addresses his words in 1 Corinthians 8-10? It is difficult to identify them exactly. Traditionally the "weak" have been understood to be Jewish Christians while the "strong" were thought to be Gentile Christians. Certainly Jews had a strong sense of dietary prohibitions and a horror of idolatry; and Gentiles who had always eaten idol-meat would see little reason to stop, especially after discovering that idols were a sham. But this interpretation cannot be correct given Paul's words in 8:7: "Some people are so accustomed to idols that when they eat such food they think of it as having been sacrificed to an idol and since their conscience is weak, it is defiled." This is not a description of a Jew. In the first century Jews had nothing at all to do with idols or idol-meat.

An interesting argument is made by one commentator (Gerd Theissen). He suggests that the dividing line is between rich and poor. The more affluent Christians (the "strong") would have business and social requirements that made it necessary for them to accept invitations to dinner parties where meat would be served, perhaps even in a pagan temple (Remember that these were the only restaurants in first-century Corinth). Consequently, these "strong" Christians ate meat and thought little of it.

On the other hand there were poor Christians who rarely ate meat at all. They could not afford it. When they did get meat it would almost always have been in the context of cult worship at a temple.

So Paul would be saying to the rich businessmen (if this construction is correct): "It is all well and good that you eat idol meat as a matter of course and think little of it. But what about the poor folk in the congregation who associate such meat with cult worship and for whom such idols are still very real? They see you eating at a temple and so they copy your example. Yet afterwards they feel guilty and defiled. Perhaps they even get drawn back into temple worship. Or worse still, this may open them up once more to demonic influence. For their sake, apart from anything else, don't eat at temples. It is okay to eat idol meat in your own home or in the homes of others. Yet even there, if someone points out that this is idol-meat, thinking that it will cause you religious offense, don't indulge."

You can see why there is such a strong reaction by the "strong." "For an Erastus (see Romans 16:23) if indeed he was the rising public servant who in a few years would be aedile (the chief magistrate or officer) in charge of all the Corinthian meat-markets, a restriction of his social intercourse to fellow Christians would mean a drastic reduction of his horizons and a disruption of his career."—Taken from *The First Urban Christians* by Wayne Meeks (Yale University Press/New Haven, Conn.), p. 69.

The Meat Market

Meat markets were a common sight throughout the Roman Empire. Archeologists have uncovered the sites of various such markets (or *marcella),* the best preserved being in Pompeii. These were enclosed areas in the middle of which stood a circular cupola on pillars where meat was displayed for sale. In one of the shops in Pompeii entire skeletons of sheep were found suggesting that meat may also have been sold "on the hoof" or that animals were actually slaughtered in the *marcellum* itself.

A *marcellum* has been located in the excavation of Corinth. It was one of a row of shops facing on to an open space paved with a mosaic floor.

The word *marcellum* is, in fact, not a Greek word at all but comes from the Latin. It is only one of four Latin words that Paul uses in his writings (the others are "cloak" and "parchment" in 2 Timothy 4:13 and "palace guard" in Philippians 1:13).

Temples

Suppose you are living in first-century Corinth. You are a newly converted Christian, and one day you receive the following invitation: "Chaeremon invites you to dine at the table of the lord Serapis in the Serapeum, tomorrow the 15th, at the ninth hour." (This invitation was found amongst some Egyptian papyri. Serapis was a god worshiped in one of the mystery cults and his temple was called the Serapeum. There were two Serapeum in Corinth.)

Would you attend?

On the positive side, such dinner parties were common in the first century. The temples served as the only restaurants in those days. So friends invited one another to temple banquets.

The problem was, and this is the negative side, these were seldom simple, private little dinner parties, off in a candle-lit corner of the temple. These were public banquets which served as part of a worship service. On special occasions such as births and weddings or at times of the seasonal feasts, friends would go up together to the temple. There they would offer large quantitites of food as a sacrifice. Some of this food went to the priests; another portion was burned before the god in his honor; while the rest was prepared for the worshiper and his friends.

The service did not stop when the meal was concluded. In many cults, worship ended with ritual prostitution involving the priestesses and guests. In other words, the banquet ended in a sacred orgy. . . .

So . . . would you accept your friends Chaeremon's invitation?—(This material was adapted from *Corinthians, A Study Guide* by Gordon Fee [Brussels: International Correspondence Institute, 1979] pp. 144-145)

UNIT 17—Propriety in Worship/1 Corinthians 11:2-16

TEXT

Propriety in Worship

²I praise you for remembering me in everything and for holding to the teachings, just as I passed them on to you.

³Now I want you to realize that the head of every man is Christ, and the head of the woman is man, and the head of Christ is God. ⁴Every man who prays or prophesies with his head covered dishonors his head. ⁵And every woman who prays or prophesies with her head uncovered dishonors her head—it is just as though her head were shaved. ⁶If a woman does not cover her head, she should have her hair cut off; and if it is a disgrace for a woman to have her hair cut or shaved off, she should cover her head. ⁷A man ought not to cover his head, since he is the image and glory of God; but the woman is the glory of man. ⁸For man did not come from woman, but woman from man; ⁹neither was man created for woman, but woman for man. ¹⁰For this reason, and because of the angels, the woman ought to have a sign of authority on her head.

¹¹In the Lord, however, woman is not independent of man, nor is man independent of woman. ¹²For as woman came from man, so also man is born of woman. But everything comes from God. ¹³Judge for yourselves: Is it proper for a woman to pray to God with her head uncovered? ¹⁴Does not the very nature of things teach you that if a man has long hair, it is a disgrace to him, ¹⁵but that if a woman has long hair, it is her glory? For long hair is given to her as a covering. ¹⁶If anyone wants to be contentious about this, we have no other practice—nor do the churches of God.

ᵃ Or traditions   ᵇ4-7 Or ⁴Every man who prays or prophesies with long hair dishonors his head. ⁵And every woman who prays or prophesies with no covering of hair on her head dishonors her head—she is just like one of the "shorn women." ⁶If a woman has no covering, let her be for now with short hair, but since it is a disgrace for a woman to have her hair shorn or shaved, she should grow it again. ⁷A man ought not to have long hair

STUDY

READ

First Reading/First Impressions
My first reaction to this passage is:

Second Reading/Big Idea
What are two or three questions this passage raises for you?

SEARCH

1. Chapters 11-14 deal with issues related to behavior in public worship. This passage is very difficult because of uncertainty about the text itself (see footnote), whether Paul at points is quoting (and then refuting) arguments the Corinthians have put forward, and just what were the cultural standards of propriety of women in public! In light of these uncertainties, what do the Corinthians seem to be doing wrong in this instance?

2. Reading between the lines, what problems are being created by the women doing things differently here than were being done in other churches?

3. Paul deals with this issue of women wearing veils (or having long hair—see textual footnote) in worship considering both theological and cultural arguments. In the first box, jot down the theological arguments he uses, and in the second the cultural ones (e.g., those reasons he puts forth without any reference to the Old Testament or to God).

4. What questions do the arguments raise for you?

5. Does the fact that "head" in verse 3 means "source or origin" rather than "ruler" (see notes) make a difference in how you understand this passage? How?

6. Do you think verses 11-12 support or undermine the view that head-covering is a permanent need for women in church? Why?

APPLY

Concern for the glory of God (vv. 3, 12), the interdependence of men and women (vv. 11-12), and sensitivity to cultural sensibilities (vv. 5, 13-16) seem to be three major principles that emerge here guiding decisions about what is appropriate in worship. Given the heated discussions today about the role of women in the church, what insights about this issue from here would be appropriate in your Christian circles?

GROUP AGENDA

Divide into groups of 4 before you start to share. And follow the time recommendations.

TO BEGIN/10 Minutes (Choose 1 or 2)

☐ What was the hair style when you were a teenager? ☐ If you *had* to wear a hat, what kind of hat would you choose to wear? What kind of hat would you pick for the person on your right--to match their personality--such as a fishing hat, Easter bonnet, football helmet, African safari pith helmet, old fashioned gingham bonnet, etc.? ☐ What did you jot down under READ in your study?

TO GO DEEPER/20 Minutes (Choose 2 or 3)

☐ Share the SEARCH questions in the Bible study, one person taking number 1, the next person taking number 2, etc. ☐ What do you know about the treatment of women in the first century? ☐ In light of the historical context, would it be an overstatement to say that Paul (and the Christian church) did more for "equal rights" than anyone has done in the last two thousand years? ☐ Case History: Liz, a close friend, is a highly respected lawyer in your town. She is very much drawn to Christ because of his emphasis on love, peace, and justice. But passages like this make her very cautious about embracing the faith. How would you counsel her?

TO CLOSE/5-20 Minutes (choose 1 or 2)

☐ What did you put down for APPLY? ☐ Some Christians today practice head-covering, and some don't. What would you do if you moved to a community where the practice was just the opposite of that with which you are familiar? ☐ Many things in our worship life reflect the culture we live in (i.e., style of dress, music, length of meeting, etc.). How do you discern between when a cultural practice is OK and when it is really a hindrance to worship?

NOTES ON 1 CORINTHIANS 11:2-16

Summary . . . Paul tackles yet another question raised in the letter sent him by the Corinthians (7:1): the veiling of women. This is the first of a series of problems (spanning chapters 11-14) related to conduct at worship services. This section is *not* about wives submitting to husbands or women trying to act like men. Such misunderstanding may arise since Paul's argument here is notoriously difficult to follow. "This is because he is convinced that the women should continue the prevailing custom (of wearing veils). But to get them to do so he must give some good reasons. Therefore, the argument fluctuates from one reason to another, but not in clearly distinguishable paragraphs" (Fee).

v. 2 **I praise you** . . . Paul has been forced to say some hard things to the Corinthian Christians but he is by no means unequivocally negative towards them. Whenever possible he praises them. Here, specifically, he praises them for thinking kindly of him (perhaps only a portion of the church chafed under his "restrictions" or perhaps he is being slightly tongue-in-cheek here). He also praises them for adhering to basic Christian teaching.

teachings . . . The New Testament had not been compiled by this time in history and so evangelists instructed their converts by word-of-mouth as to the nature of the gospel and as to the way one should live as a Christian. Paul refers here to these basic precepts or "traditions" (the literal translation of the word). In verse 17, however, it is clear that the Corinthians did not keep all the traditions. It is also clear in verses 3-16 that they were breaking another tradition—the wearing of veils. Paul may be quoting from their letter in which they assure him that they are "keeping all the traditions" when, in fact, the women had discarded veils, or at least were thinking of doing so.

v. 3 **head** . . . This is the key word in this section, used some 12 times. The difficulty is that Paul sometimes uses the word literally (referring to the physical head, with hair, eyes, mouth, etc.—i.e., in verses 4a, 5a, 5c, 6, 7, 10). However, in verse 3 "head" is used metaphorically. And in verse 4b and verse 5b it is not clear which sense is intended (though it is probably metaphorical)! Such word-play is not unusual in Paul's writings.

The head of the woman is man . . . While today (and in the Old Testament) "head" might be understood to mean "the ruler of a community," in Greek when the word is used metaphorically it means "origin," as in the "source (head) of a river." What Paul has in mind here (as is clear from verses 8-9) is Genesis 2:18-23—the creation of the first woman from Adam the first man. Woman has her *origins* in man. Had Paul wanted to convey the idea of man ruling over woman he would have used a different Greek word (Barrett).

The head of Christ is God . . . God is the origin and therefore the explanation of Christ's being, just as Christ is the creating agent of all people.

v. 4 **prophesies** . . . Paul will discuss the gift of prophecy in 12:10f.

with his head covered . . . The literal translation is: "with (something hanging) down from his head" and most likely refers to a veil that covered the whole head down to the shoulders such as respectable Jewish and Roman women wore in public. It does *not* refer to a hat or kerchief. In fact, it was the custom for Jewish *men,* not women, to wear a small cap when at worship.

dishonors his head . . . Probably this second use of "head" is metaphorical and refers to Christ. A man with his head covered dishonors Christ.

v. 5 **with her head uncovered** . . . It is difficult to know exactly the nature of the local custom, but what is clear is that women were participating actively in public worship (praying and prophesying); that they were doing so without a veil; and that this was offensive. Note that Paul does not forbid participation by women in worship. If this were wrong in and of itself, he would have simply told them to stop. He would not have wasted time telling them to wear veils.

dishonors her head . . . probably, as in verse 4, where the second use of "head" is metaphorical, so too is it here. A woman shames her husband when she is unveiled during worship.

v. 6 . . . Since Paul understands that nature dictates a covering of hair for a woman (vv. 14-15); it is as unnatural an act for her to go without a veil as it is for her to have her hair shaved off. This argument is cultural in nature. In the same way that she would be disgraced by shaving off her hair, she is disgraced by not having a veil when praying and prophesying. Paul's argument is, as Chrysostom put it: "If you throw off the veil imposed by the law, throw off that imposed by nature too."

v. 7 ... Arguing from the order of origin in verse 3, here Paul gives his conclusion as it applies to the idea of veils. "Men should *not be covered* in divine worship because that would cover 'Christ's glory,' which is seen in man. And Christ's glory *should* be seen. But the wife should *be covered* because to be *uncovered* would mean to reflect 'man's glory,' which is seen in women. And one should not call attention to the creature in the presence of the Creator in worship" (Fee).

vv. 8-9 ... Paul explains in what sense *the woman is the glory of man.*

v. 10 **For this reason** ... This refers back to verse 7 (vv. 8-9 are parenthetical). The reason why a woman is to wear a veil is because man's glory should not be exposed during worship, as he explained in verse 7. He also offers two more reasons why a woman should wear a veil (because of angels and because it is a sign of her new authority).

because of the angels ... Angels were seen as the "guardians of the created order" and as such would be offended by this "lapse from due order."

a sign of authority ... Since now a woman as well as a man " 'speaks to God in prayer and declares his word in prophecy, to do so she needs authority and power from God. The headcovering which symbolizes the effacement of man's glory in the presence of God also serves as a sign of the authority which is given to the woman.' That is, her veil represents the new authority given to women under the new dispensation to do things which formerly had not been permitted her" (Hooker in Barrett).

v. 11 **however** ... In verses 11-12 Paul balances what he said in verses 8-9. Though woman came from man (she was taken from the side of Adam, Genesis 2:21) it is also true that men come from women in the natural course of childbirth. Therefore, men and women are mutually interdependent.

not independent ... While verses 2-16 do not directly examine the relationship between husband and wife, here Paul does point out the mutual interdependence that exists between men and women and their equal dependence on God.

vv. 13-15 ... Paul now argues, on the basis of the cultural norms of that day, whereby it was felt that it was proper for men to have short hair and proper for women to have long hair. Thus from the culture's point of view it was a disgrace for a woman to pray without a veil.

v. 14 **the very nature of things** ... Paul argues that men should have short hair not because "nature" dictates that male hair is short. In fact "nature" dictates that all hair grows constantly. It is culture (this is what the phrase "The very nature of things" means) that dictates that male hair ought to be cut and it is custom that dictates that shame comes when it is not.

v. 16 ... The concluding thrust of Paul's argument is: "This is the way it has always been done and to attempt otherwise is to bring dissension into the church and that clearly is not good." He seems to be saying to the church at Corinth that they ought not to call attention to themselves by disregarding this particular cultural norm.

COMMENTS

Paul's Argument

Paul argues his case for headcovering from two perspectives: the theological and the cultural. He mixes the two arguments together however. The following is an attempt to isolate the thrust of each argument by collecting together related verses and adding a few explanatory comments.

The Theological Argument:

"Now I want you to realize that the head of every man is Christ, and the head of the woman is man, and the head of Christ is God (v. 3) ... A man ought not to cover his head since he is the image and glory of God; but the woman ought to cover her head since she is the glory of man (v. 7...In the Lord, however, woman is not independent of man, nor is man independent of woman. For as woman came from man, so also man is born of woman. But everything comes from God."

The Cultural Argument

1. "Every man who prays or prophecies with his head covered dishonors his head (Christ). And every woman who prays or prophesies with her head uncovered dishonors her head (her husband)—it is just as though her head were shaved. If a woman does not cover her head, she should have her hair cut off; and if it is a disgrace for a woman to have her hair cut or shaved off, she should cover her head (vv. 4-6)."

2. "Judge for yourselves: Is it proper for a woman to pray to God with her head uncovered? Does not the very nature of things teach you that if a man has long hair, it is a disgrace to him, but that if a woman has long hair, it is her glory? For long hair is given to her as a covering (vv. 13-15).

3. "If anyone wants to be contentious about this, we have no other practice—nor do the churches of God" (v. 16).

UNIT 18—The Lord's Supper/1 Corinthians 11:17-34

TEXT

The Lord's Supper

17In the following directives I have no praise for you, for your meetings do more harm than good. 18In the first place, I hear that when you come together as a church, there are divisions among you, and to some extent I believe it. 19No doubt there have to be differences among you to show which of you have God's approval. 20When you come together, it is not the Lord's Supper you eat, 21for as you eat, each of you goes ahead without waiting for anybody else. One remains hungry, another gets drunk. 22Don't you have homes to eat and drink in? Or do you despise the church of God and humiliate those who have nothing? What shall I say to you? Shall I praise you for this? Certainly not!

23For I received from the Lord what I also passed on to you: The Lord Jesus, on the night he was betrayed, took bread, 24and when he had given thanks, he broke it and said, "This is my body, which is for you; do this in remembrance of me." 25In the same way, after supper he took the cup, saying, "This cup is the new covenant in my blood; do this, whenever you drink it, in remembrance of me." 26For whenever you eat this bread and drink this cup, you proclaim the Lord's death until he comes.

27Therefore, whoever eats the bread or drinks the cup of the Lord in an unworthy manner will be guilty of sinning against the body and blood of the Lord. 28A man ought to examine himself before he eats of the bread and drinks of the cup. 29For anyone who eats and drinks without recognizing the body of the Lord eats and drinks judgment on himself. 30That is why many among you are weak and sick, and a number of you have fallen asleep. 31But if we judged ourselves, we would not come under judgment. 32When we are judged by the Lord, we are being disciplined so that we will not be condemned with the world.

Continued on next page

STUDY

READ

First Reading/First Impressions

What impression of the Lord's Supper at Corinth do you have from this passage? ☐ A quiet, reflective time. ☐ A noisy feast, like at the pagan temples. ☐ A time where the poor were reminded of their poverty.

Second Reading/Big Idea

What tone of voice do you "hear" Paul using here? Why?

SEARCH

1. From verses 17-22, describe what you would have seen, heard and felt as you observed the Corinthians observing the Lord's Supper.

2. How did their actions during the Lord's Supper totally distort the very meaning of that meal? (Compare vv. 18-19, 22 with 10:17.)

3. Given their situation, why does Paul repeat the account of the Lord's Supper? (Compare vv. 23-25 with Luke 22:19-20.)

4. Remembrance (vv. 24, 25), proclamation (v. 26), and participation (10:16) are three realities of the Lord's Supper Paul highlights in this letter. How would you explain to a non-believer how the Lord's Supper serves to accomplish each of these things?

Remembrance

Proclamation

Participation

5. In light of the situation in verses 20-22, what does Paul mean by eating and drinking the Lord's Supper in "an unworthy manner" and "not recognizing the body of the Lord"? (vv. 27, 29)

6. Therefore, what would it mean to examine and judge oneself? (vv. 28, 31)

7. What is the alternative to this self-evaluation? (vv. 32, 34)

APPLY

Probably no church today is guilty of gluttony or drunkenness during the Lord's Supper or Mass, but what are some ways modern Christians fail to "recognize the body of the Lord" by creating distinctions between types of Christians? (Example: The unwritten "dress code" of some churches excludes those who can't afford that style; the insistence on one type of music communicates to others that "their" music cannot possibly be beautiful to God, etc.)

What are some practices in your church that, when viewed through the eyes of others in your community, automatically rules them out (i.e., think of one thing you would be embarrassed about if a non-believing friend came with you)?

What might be an alternative that would be more inclusive of the types of people in your community?

GROUP AGENDA

Divide into groups of 4 before you start to share. And follow the time recommendations.

TO BEGIN/10 Minutes (Choose 1 or 2)

☐ When you were a child, what do you remember about church suppers? ☐ Where did you go for family picnics? What do you remember that was special about these outings? ☐ What meeting or outing have you gone on lately that turned into a big disappointment? ☐ What did you jot down for READ?

TO GO DEEPER/20 Minutes (Choose 2 or 3)

☐ Go around and share the SEARCH questions in the Bible study, one person answering number 1, the next person number 2, etc. ☐ From the Old Testament (Exodus 12), and the ministry of Jesus (John 13), what are the historical roots of the Lord's Supper? ☐ How did Jesus take the Old Testament feast and make it into something more for the Christians? ☐ Case History: Your church has just started a monthly intra-church Saturday evening family sports night to help people get to know each other better. By the third month, only those who had played varsity sports in high school or college are attending because others are feeling slighted by these "stars." What do you suggest to help?

Continued on next page

---

[33]So then, my brothers, when you come together to eat, wait for each other. [34]If anyone is hungry, he should eat at home, so that when you meet together it may not result in judgment.

And when I come I will give further directions.

81

NOTES ON 1 CORINTHIANS 11:17-34

Summary... Paul turns to a second, more serious disorder in the Corinthian's worship experience—the chaos that communion had become.

v. 17 **no praise**... Despite his desire to encourage the Corinthians (v. 2), Paul has nothing to say on this issue.

more harm than good... In fact, so flawed are their communion services that they would be better off not having them. They harm, not heal.

v. 18 **In the first place**... There is no "in the second place," though in verse 34 Paul does refer to "further directions;" and in chapters 12 and 13 he does deal with other worship-related issues.

I hear... They had *not* written Paul about these disorders. Paul had heard what was going on from other sources (1:11; 16:17) and is so shocked that he can't really believe that it is as bad as reported ("to some extent I believe it").

GROUP AGENDA continued

TO CLOSE/5-20 Minutes (Choose 1 or 2)

☐ What did you write for APPLY? ☐ On a scale from 1 to 10, how important is the Lord's Supper to you? ☐ How seriously do you observe the command to "examine" yourself before you take the Lord's Supper? ☐ When you hear the words, "This is my body, which is for you; do this in remembrance of me," what do you think?

come together... The positive note in all this is that, in fact, the various Christian groups are still assembling together in one place for a shared service.

church... The Greek word translated *church* originally referred to a group of citizens from a particular town who had assembled together for a predetermined purpose. In the Greek Old Testament this word was used to describe the assembling together of God's people, and it came to have this meaning in the New Testament as well.

divisions... It seems that class distinction operated at the Lord's Supper—the rich ate abundantly while the poor were hungry. It is also quite possible that Jewish Christians ate *kosher* food by themselves apart from Gentile Christians, and that perhaps the ascetics sat apart from the libertarians, that those who followed Apollos did not mingle with those who followed Cephas; etc.

v. 19... Paul even finds some value in these factions: those who are acting in a truly Christian fashion have become quite obvious by comparison with all the others!

vv. 20-21... In Corinth the Lord's Supper was eaten in the context of a community meal—a so-called "love feast" (Jude 12). For communion to be set in this context is not at all surprising. For one thing, the Lord himself first instituted his Supper during a meal (Mark 14:12-26). For another, in Corinth it was quite common to eat a meal together in a temple as part of the worship of a god (see notes for 8:10 and 10:20).

v. 20 **not the Lord's Supper you eat**... The Corinthians have so abused the communion service that it can no longer be considered to be held in honor of the Lord as it was originally intended.

v. 21 **goes ahead without waiting for anybody else**... Apparently the poor were actually being excluded from the Lord's Supper (v. 33). It is conjectured that the "nobodies" who made up much of the church (1:26) were in fact slaves (7:20-24) and so simply did not have the freedom to get to church when they wanted to and the others just weren't waiting for them (Fee).

hungry... The rich were not sharing their abundant food with the poor.

drank... Some were drinking so much wine that they even got drunk while the poor probably had little to drink.

v. 22... If the rich can't wait to indulge in their food and drink, at least they should do this at home and not demean the common meal at church.

humiliate those who have nothing... The poor feel ashamed that they can't bring the abundant food and drink they see the rich eating. Paul's point is that God accepts the poor, so the rich ought not to make them feel unworthy.

vv. 23-26... Paul's first step in dealing with what is clearly an unacceptable situation is by recalling for them how Jesus instituted the Lord's Supper; his point being that these words and acts of the Lord provide the pattern for how the Corinthians should conduct their communion service (see Matthew 26:26-28; Mark 14:22-24; Luke 22:19-20).

v. 23 on the night he was betrayed ... The significance of what Jesus did at the Last Supper comes in the context of *when* it took place—immediately prior to his crucifixion.

v. 24 thanks ... There is nothing unusual in this act. The head of each Jewish household would have done the same thing.

This is my body ... Then Jesus interprets for the disciples the new meaning he is giving to these ordinary acts. He himself will become the Passover lamb for them, slain for their sins.

in remembrance ... Paul repeats this phrase twice so as to stress that the Lord's Supper is a memorial feast (Luke 22:19).

v. 25 in my blood ... The shedding of Jesus' blood inaugurates a new covenant (agreement) between God and people by which their sins are forgiven as a result of Christ's death in their place.

v. 26 ... This statement is not found in the Gospels. It is Paul's own summary of the meaning of the Lord's Supper.

proclaim the Lord's death ... The Lord's Supper *proclaims* the fact and meaning of Jesus' death in several ways: the broken bread and out-poured wine symbolically proclaim his death; the words spoken at such a meal (both formally and informally) recall the crucifixion; and the whole event itself "proclaims" his atoning death. This is why the abuses by the Corinthians are so appalling. Added together, they proclaimed a different and quite false gospel.

until he comes ... In this way Christians continue to recall the story of Jesus' death up until the time he returns again *(until he comes).* "There is little doubt that Paul, when he wrote 1 Corinthians, expected that he would live to see this event. The church as it met round the supper table would form a living link between the beginning and the end of the interim between the two comings of the Lord" (Barrett).

vv. 27-34 ... The problem Paul addresses has two parts: the vertical and the horizontal. "The vertical part of the problem was their failure to honor the Lord. The horizontal part of the problem was their failure to eat the meal as a loving community" (Fee). Paul has just dealt with the vertical (theological) problem in verses 23-26. Now in verses 27-34 he deals with the horizontal (relational) problem which he outlined in verses 17-23.

v. 27 in an unworthy manner ... What Paul is referring to here are the disorders in community behavior detailed in verses 18-22.

v. 28 examine himself ... Christians ought to scrutinize their lives to see if they are guilty of divisiveness, of lack of love, of gluttony and drunkenness (i.e., the Corinthian disorders) that might reflect negatively on *"the body and blood of the Lord."* Moral perfection is not required, simply moral scrutiny.

v. 29 without recognizing ... In fact, when the Agape Supper turned into a time of drunkenness, division, and gluttony, people lost sight of the real meaning of the bread and wine.

the body of the Lord ... "The words 'of the Lord' are almost certainly not in the original text. They are missing from the best early manuscripts. By their abuse of the Lord's Supper they were not recognizing the Lord as present with them at the Supper. But the more visible expression of their abuse has been in 'despising the church,' Paul's omission of 'of the Lord,' therefore, makes it highly probable that he intended the Corinthians to hear it both ways ... (referring) both to the body of the Lord represented in the bread and to His body the church represented in their all eating of the one loaf" (Fee).

v. 30 ... Paul contends that the *judgment* in verse 29 works itself out in concrete, physical ways. "Those who abused the Lord's table were exposing themselves to the power of demons, who were taken to be the cause of physical disease. This verse is first an explanation of events known to be taking place in Corinth, and secondly a threat directed against those who continued to misuse the Supper" (Barrett).

v. 30 fallen asleep ... died.

v. 32 ... This judgment may not, in the end, turn out to be so bad, because disipline yields growth.

vv. 33-34 ... In these exhortations Paul sums up verses 17-32.

v. 34 further directions ... Paul has apparently dealt with only the most serious problems connected with the celebration of the Lord's Supper. The other areas can wait until his visit.

UNIT 19—Spiritual Gifts/1 Corinthians 12:1-11

TEXT

Spiritual Gifts

12 Now about spiritual gifts, brothers, I do not want you to be ignorant. ²You know that when you were pagans, somehow or other you were influenced and led astray to dumb idols. ³Therefore I tell you that no one who is speaking by the Spirit of God says, "Jesus be cursed," and no one can say, "Jesus is Lord," except by the Holy Spirit.

⁴There are different kinds of gifts, but the same Spirit. ⁵There are different kinds of service, but the same Lord. ⁶There are different kinds of working, but the same God works all of them in all men.

⁷Now to each one the manifestation of the Spirit is given for the common good. ⁸To one there is given through the Spirit the message of wisdom, to another the message of knowledge by means of the same Spirit, ⁹to another faith by the same Spirit, to another gifts of healing by that one Spirit, ¹⁰to another miraculous powers, to another prophecy, to another the ability to distinguish between spirits, to another the ability to speak in different kinds of tongues, and to still another the interpretation of tongues. ¹¹All these are the work of one and the same Spirit, and he gives them to each man, just as he determines.

ᵃ10 Or *languages*; also in verse 28

STUDY

READ

First Reading/First Impressions
Put what you see as the most important verse here in your own words.

Second Reading/Big Idea
What seem to be key words in this passage?

SEARCH

1. Given verse 3, what do you imagine might have been happening in the Corinthian worship services?

2. Look at 10:19-20. What was really going on in the ecstatic speech they experienced as pagans?

3. Therefore, why is the content rather than the experience of the speech most important? (12:3)

4. What is the role of each member of the Trinity in relationship to gifts? (vv. 4-6)

5. Why does he accent this unity in the Trinity before really getting into the diversity of gifts?

6. Since the Corinthians tended towards spiritual pride (1:12; 4:8; 5:2), how might verse 7 surprise them?

7. List the nine gifts mentioned in verses 8-10.

8. What truths about the gifts are emphasized in verse 11?

APPLY

Regardless of your church's doctrinal position, what attitudes toward spiritual gifts dominate? □ Only the pastor has them. □ All believers have them, but we just keep them to ourselves. □ The goal of ministry is to free people to use their gifts for the good of others. □ Some of the gifts no longer operate today. □ The spiritual gifts for each person are only given at conversion. □ All Christians have the potential to exercise all the gifts. □ One gift, namely _____, is really the most important one. □ The more spiritual a person is, the more gifts he or she has. □ Other views: _____

Write out a summary of what you see in this passage about the origin and purpose of spiritual gifts.

Of the sample gifts listed here (see notes for descriptions), does any have your name on it? How so?

GROUP AGENDA

Divide into groups of 4 before you start to share. And follow the time recommendations.

TO BEGIN/10 Minutes (Choose 1 or 2)

□ What is one thing you do really well? □ What is one thing you would *like* to do really well? □ What was the best surprise gift you remember getting as a child? □ What did you jot down after READ?

TO GO DEEPER/20 Minutes (Choose 2 or 3)

□ Go over the SEARCH portion of the Bible study, one question at a time. □ What are two or three biblical principles in this passage on the subject of spiritual gifts that you need to remember? □ What is the nature of each gift—how would you explain it in your own words? How does each contribute to "the common good"? □ Compare and contrast the gift list in verses 8-10 with the five other lists in this section (12:28; 12:29-30; 13:1-3; 14:6 and 14:26). Which gift is found in each list? Why? □ Case History: When your church tried to recruit some more Sunday School teachers, your friend Bob shied away because he felt he had "nothing to offer." This has been his response to a number of mission needs in your church. He has a real love for God, but it does not seem to lead anywhere. What would you like him to see and how would you go about it?

TO CLOSE/5-20 Minutes (Choose 1 or 2)

□ What did you write for APPLY? □ What could we do to help one another in our group and church to exercise our spiritual gifts? □ Where do you see your gifts being used most in the service of God? □ What percent of your spiritual gifts are you presently using for the service of God?

NOTES ON 1 CORINTHIANS 12:1-11

Section Summary ... In chapters 12-14, Paul deals with the third and final issue related to the worship experience of the Corinthian church: the abuse of the gift of tongues. In his six lists of spiritual gifts (12:8-10; 12:28; 12:29-30; 13:1-3; 14:6; 14:26), his clear preoccupation is with tongues. (He mentions this gift 14 times and it is the only gift to appear in all six lists.) Apparently the Corinthians felt that people were "spiritual" (2:13, 15; 3:1) if they spoke a lot in tongues in public. In contradistinction, Paul will argue that the "greatest gift" is that which "edifies" the church, not that which, like tongues, edifies only oneself (chapter 14). Furthermore, it is "love" (chapter 13) that energizes all the gifts.

Unit Summary ... Paul's emphasis in 12:1-11 is on the variety of gifts given by the Spirit, over against the Corinthians' preoccupation with one particular gift.

v. 1 **now about** ... Paul responds to yet another concern voiced in their letter.

vv. 2-3 ... Paul contrasts pagan and Christian ecstasy. The difference is not the experience of ecstasy but *who* inspires the ecstasy—the Holy Spirit or another (demonic) spirit. The identity of the inspiring source is known by the *content* of the utterance. The Holy Spirit exalts Jesus Christ.

v. 2 **influenced and led astray** ... The image is of the ecstasy within pagan religion where one was possessed (or thought to be) and "carried away" by a supernatural being.

dumb idols ... The idols in themselves were nothing; they were silent (they could not answer prayer) but behind them lay very real demonic powers.

v. 3 **speaking by** ... The idea is of speech directly inspired by the Spirit of God. The question is *not* whether such ecstatic speech occurs (Paul assumes that it does) but what is the *content* of the speech. "Not the manner but the content of ecstatic speech determines its authenticity" (Barrett).

cursed ... Literally *anathema* or accursed.

"Jesus be cursed" ... It is not clear who would have uttered such words or under what conditions.

Jesus is Lord ... To be able to confess that one is the servant of Jesus who is indeed Lord (Master, King) of the universe is a sign of the Holy Spirit at work. "Inspiration as a religious phenomenon is in itself indifferent, and gains significance only in the context of Christian obedience" (Barrett).

vv. 4-6 ... Paul points out that not all Christians have the same gift (nor every gift), nor do they render the same service. However, all gifts spring from the same Spirit; are used to serve the same Lord; and are all energized by the power of the same God. (This is an early statement of the Trinity.)

v. 4 **gifts** ... See the note for 1:7.

v. 5 **service** ... The purpose of the gifts is to serve and aid others in various ways; yet all is done in the name of and for the sake of the same Lord.

v. 6 **working** ... The Greek root is *energeia* ("energy") and refers to the various ways in which God's *power* is displayed because, indeed, it is God's power operating in the gifts.

v. 7 **to each one** ... *Every* Christian has a spiritual gift.

for the common good ... The purpose of these gifts is not private advantage but community growth.

vv. 8-10 ... Paul illustrates the variety of gifts. By chapter 14 it will have become clear that he stresses this point because the Corinthians had become preoccupied, to their detriment, with a single gift—tongues.

v. 8 **through the Spirit** ... Paul again emphasizes the supernatural origins of these gifts.

wisdom/knowledge ... It is not clear how (or if) these gifts differ. Perhaps a *message of wisdom* focused on practical, ethical instruction while a *message of knowledge* involved exposition of biblical truth. In either case the emphasis is on the actual discourse given for the benefit of the assembled Christians.

v.9 **faith** ... A special ability "to claim from God extraordinary manifestations of power in the natural world" (Barrett). Saving faith, which all Christians share, is not in view here.

healing ... The special ability to effect miraculous cures. Paul apparently had this gift (Acts 14:8-10).

COMMENTS

v. 10 **miraculous powers** . . . Probably the gift of exorcism and similar types of confrontation with evil supernatural powers.

prophecy . . . Inspired utterances given in ordinary (not ecstatic) speech, distinguished from teaching and wisdom by its unpremeditated nature (see chapter 14).

distinguish between spirits . . . Just because a person *claimed* to be inspired by the Holy Spirit did not make it true. Those who possessed this gift of discernment were able to identify the *source* of an utterance—whether it came from the Holy Spirit or from another spirit.

tongues . . . Ecstatic speech, unintelligible except by those with the gift of *interpretation of tongues* (see 13:1; chapter 14).

UNIT 20—One Body, Many Parts/1 Corinthians 12:12-31

TEXT

One Body, Many Parts

¹²The body is a unit, though it is made up of many parts; and though all its parts are many, they form one body. So it is with Christ. ¹³For we were all baptized by one Spirit into one body—whether Jews or Greeks, slave or free—and we were all given the one Spirit to drink.

¹⁴Now the body is not made up of one part but of many. ¹⁵If the foot should say, "Because I am not a hand, I do not belong to the body," it would not for that reason cease to be part of the body. ¹⁶And if the ear should say, "Because I am not an eye, I do not belong to the body," it would not for that reason cease to be part of the body. ¹⁷If the whole body were an eye, where would the sense of hearing be? If the whole body were an ear, where would the sense of smell be? ¹⁸But in fact God has arranged the parts in the body, every one of them, just as he wanted them to be. ¹⁹If they were all one part, where would the body be? ²⁰As it is, there are many parts, but one body.

²¹The eye cannot say to the hand, "I don't need you!" And the head cannot say to the feet, "I don't need you!" ²²On the contrary, those parts of the body that seem to be weaker are indispensable, ²³and the parts that we think are less honorable we treat with special honor. And the parts that are unpresentable are treated with special modesty, ²⁴while our presentable parts need no special treatment. But God has combined the members of the body and has given greater honor to the parts that lacked it, ²⁵so that there should be no division in the body, but that its parts should have equal concern for each other. ²⁶If one part suffers, every part suffers with it; if one part is honored, every part rejoices with it.

²⁷Now you are the body of Christ, and each one of you is a part of it. ²⁸And in the church God has appointed first of all apostles, second prophets, third teachers, then workers of

Continued on next page

STUDY

READ

First Reading/First Impressions
What are two or three key words here?

Second Reading/Big Idea
If you were an editor for Reader's Digest, how would you condense this into one or two sentences?

SEARCH

1. In verses 12-13, in what ways does Paul stress the unity of the believers?

2. Having established the basis for unity, what is Paul's purpose in verses 14-20?

3. Verses 15-21 present an absurd picture (One that Gary Larson who draws "The Far Side" cartoons could get off on!) Try your hand at drawing a cartoon capturing the absurdity Paul illustrates here.

4. How does Paul counter their tendency towards spiritual pride in verses 21-26?

5. From what Paul is saying, what do you think must have been the situation in the church in Corinth?

6. How could you illustrate the truth of verse 26 from your own body? Your church?

7. List all the different gifts in verses 28-30.

8. What two categories of "gifts" do you find in this list?

APPLY

If you had to pass out some Academy Awards to people who have contributed their own spiritual gifts to your life as part of the "body of Christ," who would you nominate for special recognition in these categories:

APOSTLE: (One who planted the message of Christ in you) _____

PROPHET: (One who opened up new implications of the faith for you) _____

TEACHER: (One who instructed and established you in the faith) _____

WORKER OF MIRACLES: (One who believed God for great things) _____

GIFT OF HEALING: (One who was there when you were hurting) _____

GIFT OF ADMINISTRATION: (One who helped you discipline your life) _____

GROUP AGENDA

Divide into groups of 4 before you start to share. And follow the time recommendations.

TO BEGIN/10 Minutes (Choose 1 or 2)

☐ What do you like most about your body? ☐ If you were in charge of designing a revolutionary new human body, what would you change? ☐ What is the most unified body you have ever been a part of (a team, an Army unit, a fraternity, etc)? What made this group so unified? What did you accomplish together? ☐ What did you jot down under READ in your study?

TO GO DEEPER/20 Minutes (Choose 2 or 3)

☐ Share what you jotted down under SEARCH in your Bible study, one question at a time. ☐ In your own words, what is Paul trying to teach the Corinthians in this passage? What other illustration could you use to make the same points? ☐ In the church today, of the various parts of the "body," which part do you think is overdeveloped? Which one is underdeveloped? ☐ Case History: At 3 o'clock in the morning you get a call from an old college friend. He has to make a decision whether to go for ordination into the priesthood. He enrolled in seminary to make his mother happy. Now, he is having second thoughts about his motives. He asks for your advice.

Continued on next page

miracles, also those having gifts of healing, those able to help others, those with gifts of administration, and those speaking in different kinds of tongues. [29]Are all apostles? Are all prophets? Are all teachers? Do all work miracles? [30]Do all have gifts of healing? Do all speak in tongues? Do all interpret? [31]But eagerly desire the greater gifts.

[a]13 Or with; or in   [b]30 Or other languages   [c]31 Or But you are eagerly desiring

NOTES ON 1 CORINTHIANS 12:12-31

Summary . . . Having pointed out the *diversity* of gifts in 12:1-11 (thus drawing the Corinthians away from their preoccupation with one gift—tongues), now Paul examines the *unity* that exists within all this diversity. Once having established that Christians are all part of one body (vv. 12-13), Paul returns then to the idea of diversity, in which he not only points out the variety of gifts that exist, but the fact that none are inferior and all are necessary.

v. 12 **a unit . . . made up of many parts** . . . This is Paul's central point in verses 12-30: "diversity within unity" (Fee).

So it is with Christ . . . The church is the body of Christ (v. 27) and so indeed Christ can be understood to be made up of many parts. Yet he is also the Lord (v. 3) and thus head over that church.

v. 13 . . . Here Paul points to the *unity* side of the body of Christ. Unity exists because *all* are baptized into one Spirit and *all* drink from one Spirit. His concern is not with

---

GROUP AGENDA continued

TO CLOSE/5-20 Minutes (Choose 1 or 2)

☐ What did you jot down for APPLY in your study? ☐ If you had to compare how you see yourself to one of the parts of a body, which part would you be (a hand, a mouth, an ear, etc.)? Which part of the body do you need most for your own help right now? ☐ If you had to grade your Bible study group on how well you worked together—on a scale from 1 to 10—what would it be? ☐ How much does it concern you that there are other members of the body of Christ—even in your own church—who are out of work, without enough food, shelter or clothes?

how people become believers but with how believers become one body. The term "baptism" is probably metaphorical (Fee). The way believers are "put into one Spirit" is like baptism; i.e., "think of it as being immersed in the Spirit."

baptized by one Spirit . . . In fact, the footnoted translation of the preposition is probably the correct rendering; i.e., the phrase should read "baptized *in* one Spirit" since Paul's concern is not with the means *by which* believers are baptized but with the common reality *in which* all believers exist, i.e., the Holy Spirit (Fee).

Jews or Greeks, slave or free . . . See Galatians 3:28.

one Spirit to drink . . . Paul continues speaking metaphorically, with the idea of water still dominant. Being incorporated into one body is not only like baptism, it is also like "drinking the same Spirit."

v. 14 . . . Now Paul points to the *diversity* side of the body of Christ (which is his major concern): the one body has many different parts to it—which his analogy will demonstrate.

vv. 15-26 . . . Having established that all Christians are part of one body (which is, in fact, Christ's body) and that this body has a variety of parts, Paul then develops an elaborate metaphor based on the human body out of which he makes two points: There are a variety of gifts (vv. 15-20) and each gift is vital regardless of its nature (vv. 21-26).

vv. 15-20 . . . Paul's point is that it is just as ludicrous for Christians to opt out of the body of Christ (presumably by not using their gifts during worship) because they have one gift and not another (presumably more desired) gift, as it is for a foot (or ear) to decide not to be part of a physical body because it is not a hand (or eye).

v. 17 . . . If all Christians had the same gift, the body would be impoverished.

vv. 21-26 . . . Just as it is presumptive of the eye (or head) to say to the hand (or feet) that it has no need of it, so too, a Christian ought not to deny the value, need, or function of anyone's spiritual gift, especially on the basis that it is different from, or inferior to, one's own gift.

v. 21 . . . Each part of the body *needs* the others. No one gift (e.g., tongues) can stand alone. Wholeness requires all the parts functioning together.

v. 22 **weaker** . . . "The delicate organs, such as the eye; and the invisible organs such as the heart" (Barrett).

v. 26 . . . In fact, the *whole person* suffers when one (to use a modern example) sprains an ankle. It is not just the ankle that suffers.

v. 27 . . . Paul sums up the meaning of his metaphor.

the body of Christ . . . By this phrase Paul conveys the idea *not* that Christ consists of this body; but that Christ rules over this body and that this body belongs to Him.

v. 28 . . . Paul offers a second list of the types of gifts given by the Holy Spirit (see the parallel list in Ephesians 4:11)—mixing

COMMENTS

together ministries (e.g., apostles) with *charismata* proper (e.g., the gift of healing).

apostles ... (see note 9:5). These individuals were responsible for founding new churches. They were pioneer church starters.

prophets ... Those who were inspired to speak God's word to the church, in plain (not ecstatic) language. See chapter 14.

teachers ... Those gifted to instruct others in the meaning of the Christian faith and its implications for one's lifestyle.

then ... Having first focused on those gifts whereby the church is established and nurtured, Paul then shifts to other gifts.

to help others ... The gift of support; those whose function it was to aid the needy, e.g., the poor, the widow, the orphan.

administration ... The gift of direction (literally the process of steering a ship through the rocks and safely to shore): those whose function it was to guide church affairs.

vv. 29-30 ... While Paul does not rule out the fact that a particular individual might possess more than one gift, he is quite clear that not everybody has all gifts. The implied answer to each question is "No."

v. 31 ... Paul establishes the context within which all gifts should function: love, which is the more excellent way.

The Gift of ...
by Peter Wagner

Prophecy
The gift of prophecy is the special ability that God gives to certain members of the Body of Christ to receive and communicate an immediate message of God to His people through a divinely-anointed utterance.

Since the word "prophecy" today usually means predicting the future, it is difficult for some people to realize that the biblical use of the word includes not only the future but also a word for the present. In fact the gift of prophecy has been used much more for dealing with present situations than with future events. The meaning of the Greek word is basically "to speak forth" or "to speak for another." Those who have the gift of prophecy receive personal inspiration as to God's purpose in a concrete situation. God speaks through the prophet.

Miracles
The gift of miracles is the special ability that God gives to certain members of the Body of Christ to serve as human intermediaries through whom it pleases God to perform powerful acts that are perceived by observers to have altered the ordinary course of nature.

Notice that this definition does not close the door to the performance of miracles that may later be "disproved" by the application of Western scientific methodologies. I have read lengthy explanations, for example, of why people who were raised from the dead in Indonesia were not really raised from the dead. Some Western investigators apparently went to Indonesia and concluded that, according to their Western definitions of death, it did not happen.

This would be amusing if it were not so pathetic. God performed the miracles for Indonesians, not for Americans or Europeans. If Indonesians really and truly thought, in terms of their own worldview, that the dead had been raised, the miracle happened. The ordinary course of nature had been altered. If through observing this, Indonesian believers were strengthened in their faith and Indonesian unbelievers were convinced of the power of God and became followers of Jesus Christ, the purpose of the miracle was accomplished. Even within our Western worldview the most advanced scientists and doctors of jurisprudence have not been able to agree precisely on when death actually occurs. Why, then, superimpose our inexact worldview on the Indonesians' inexact worldview?

Healing
The gift of healing is the special ability that God gives to certain members of the Body of Christ to serve as human intermediaries through whom it pleases God to cure illness and restore health apart from the use of natural means.

In one sense the gift of healing can be understood as a specialized manifestation of the gift of miracles, but the two are mentioned separately in the Bible, so we separate them also. Obviously, healing has to do with human illness specifically, although it includes all kinds of human illnesses. The biblical reference to the gift in 1 Corinthians 12:28 is literally gifts (plural) of healings (plural). This seems to imply that there are many varieties of the gift for different kinds of illnesses.

To restrict the gift of healing just to physical diseases is not proper. The gift can also be used to cure mental, emotional and spiritual illnesses. Agnes Sanford, a contemporary with the gift of healing, has the gift of "healing the memory." Another, Ruth Carter Stapleton, deals with "inner healing." There may be many more varieties.—Taken from *Your Spiritual Gifts Can Help Your Church Grow* (Regal Books), pp. 228-229, 237-240.

UNIT 21—Love/1 Corinthians 13:1-13

TEXT

Love

And now I will show you the most excellent way. **13** If I speak in the tongues of men and of angels, but have not love, I am only a resounding gong or a clanging cymbal. ²If I have the gift of prophecy and can fathom all mysteries and all knowledge, and if I have a faith that can move mountains, but have not love, I am nothing. ³If I give all I possess to the poor and surrender my body to the flames, but have not love, I gain nothing.

⁴Love is patient, love is kind. It does not envy, it does not boast, it is not proud. ⁵It is not rude, it is not self-seeking, it is not easily angered, it keeps no record of wrongs. ⁶Love does not delight in evil but rejoices with the truth. ⁷It always protects, always trusts, always hopes, always perseveres.

⁸Love never fails. But where there are prophecies, they will cease; where there are tongues, they will be stilled; where there is knowledge, it will pass away. ⁹For we know in part and we prophesy in part, ¹⁰but when perfection comes, the imperfect disappears. ¹¹When I was a child, I talked like a child, I thought like a child, I reasoned like a child. When I became a man, I put childish ways behind me. ¹²Now we see but a poor reflection; then we shall see face to face. Now I know in part; then I shall know fully, even as I am fully known.

¹³And now these three remain: faith, hope and love. But the greatest of these is love.

[a] 1 Or *languages*   [b] 3 Some early manuscripts *body that I may boast*

STUDY

READ

First Reading/First Impressions
A good title for this "love song" would be:

Second Reading/Big Idea
What to you is the "best verse" in this passage? Why?

SEARCH

1. Given the Corinthians' quest for spiritual gifts and power, what is Paul's point in verses 1-3?

2. Paraphrase what he says in verses 1-3 using one of the strengths you see in yourself.

3. What is love? List the 7 characteristics that love "is" and the 8 characteristics that love "is not." (vv. 4-7)

LOVE IS	LOVE IS NOT

4. What is the significance of the contrast he makes between gifts and love in verses 8-12?

5. Why will spiritual gifts cease to be relevant? (vv. 11-12)

6. What three things carry over into the new age? (v. 13)

APPLY

This exercise will take some time, but will be very profitable. Using this as an example of practically applying what "Love is patient" means, rewrite each of the "love is . . ." qualities to show what love ought to look like in your life at home, work, political views, church, etc.

> *Love will not blow its top when things go wrong — even though my kid borrows my screwdriver for the fifth time in a week and loses it — love will not take out its anger on my kid.*

Be honest to the verse, whether you are this way or not!

Then take the next phrase: *"Love is kind,"* and rewrite this, etc. When you are through, you should have verse 4 in your own everyday language and everyday situation. "Love is patient, love is kind. It does not envy, it does not boast, it is not proud."

GROUP AGENDA

Divide into groups of 4 before you start to share. And follow the time recommendations.

TO BEGIN/10 Minutes (Choose 1 or 2)

☐ What did you put down for READ? ☐ As a teenager, what was your favorite love song? Why? ☐ Who in your life best exemplifies what real love is all about? Why? ☐ If I wanted to "test your patience," what would be a way I could really find out how short a fuse you had? Put you in a traffic jam? A long grocery line? Have the baby keep on crying? Be consistently late? What?

TO GO DEEPER/20 Minutes (Choose 2 or 3)

☐ Share the SEARCH portion of the Bible study, one person sharing question 1, the next person number 2, etc. ☐ One Bible scholar has said that Paul was able to write eloquently about love because of his own struggle to be a loving person. How do you feel about this? Do you think that certain people are naturally more loving than others? What is the difference between being "naturally loving" and the love that Paul is talking about? ☐ Case History: Fred has had it. After at first ignoring them, his co-workers continue to make racial innuendos pointed at him. He feels like he has to take some action, but doesn't want to just give in to anger. What might be a way for him to exercise love without allowing their hurtful prejudice to go unchallenged?

TO CLOSE/5-20 Minutes (Choose 1 or 2)

☐ What did you write for your paraphrases in APPLY? ☐ When, if ever, have you been burned in a "love relationship"? What went wrong? How was the love in that relationship different from the love Paul is talking about? ☐ What have you learned about love in the past six months? ☐ How would you paraphrase the last verse in your own words?

NOTES ON 1 CORINTHIANS 13:1-13

Summary ... In this soaring hymn in praise of love (which has become a classic piece of literature) Paul first points out (vv. 1-3) the primacy of love (in contrast to other religious activities); and describes love itself (vv. 4-7) and ends (vv. 8-13) by pointing out love's enduring quality (in contrast, once again, to other religious activities). As Karl Barth outlines the chapter: "It is love alone that counts (vv. 1-3); it is love alone that triumphs (vv. 4-7); it is love alone that endures (vv. 8-13)."

vv. 1-3 ... If a person does not love, neither spiritual gifts, nor good deeds, nor martyrdom is of any ultimate value to that person. Love is the context within which these gifts and deeds become significant.

v. 1 **tongues of men and of angels** ... Ecstatic speech—highly prized in Corinth—is an authentic gift of the Holy Spirit; however, it becomes like the unintelligible noise of pagan worship when used outside the context of love.

gong/cymbal ... Paul is probably thinking of the repititious and meaningless noise generated at pagan temples by beating on metal instruments.

v. 2 ... Paul contrasts three other spiritual gifts with love: prophecy, knowledge, and faith.

prophecy ... Such activity is highly commended by Paul (e.g. 14:1); yet without love even a prophet is really nothing.

fathom all mysteries ... In Corinth special, esoteric knowledge was highly prized (1:18—2:16), but even if one knew the very secrets of God, without love it would be to no end. That which makes a person significant (i.e., the opposite of *nothing*) is not a gift like prophecy or knowledge but it is the ability to love.

faith that can move mountains ... Paul refers to Jesus' words in Mark 11:23— even such massive faith that can unleash God's power in visible ways is not enough to make a person significant without love at its foundation.

v. 3 **give all I possess to the poor** ... Presumably Paul refers to goods and property given to others but not in love. The point is not: do not give if you cannot do so in love (the poor still profit from the gifts regardless of the spirit in which they are given), but rather that the loveless giver gains no reward on the day of judgment.

surrender my body ... Not even the act of the martyr—giving up one's very life for the sake of another or in a great cause— brings personal benefit when it is done outside love.

vv. 4-7 ... By way of definition, Paul tells us what love does and does not do. He defines love in terms of action and attitude.

v. 4 **patient** ... This word describes patience with people (not circumstances). It characterizes the person who is slow to anger (long suffering) despite provocation.

kind ... In fact, the loving person does good to those who provoke him/her.

not envy ... The loving person does not covet what others have nor begrudge them their possessions.

not boast ... The loving person is self-effacing, not a braggart.

not proud ... Literally not "puffed up." The loving person does not feel others to be inferior nor does he/she look down on people.

v. 5 **not rude** ... The same (Greek) word is used in 7:36 to describe a man who led on a woman but then refused to marry her.

not self-seeking ... The loving person not only does not insist on his/her rights but will give up his/her due for the sake of others.

not easily angered ... The loving person is not easily angered by others; he/she is not touchy.

keeps no record of wrongs ... The verb is an accounting term and the image is of a ledger sheet on which wrongs received are recorded. The loving person forgives and forgets.

v. 6 **does not delight in evil** ... The loving person does not rejoice when others fail (which could make him/her feel superior) nor enjoys pointing out wrong in others.

rejoices with the truth ... Paul shifts back to the positive.

v. 7 **trusts** ... Literally "believes all things" i.e., "never loses faith."

hopes ... Love does not lose hope.

COMMENTS

perseveres ... Love keeps loving despite hardship.

vv. 8-12 ... Having described love, Paul once again contrasts love with spiritual gifts, emphasizing this time the permanent quality of love over against the transitory nature of the *charismata*.

v. 8 **love never fails** ... In the sense that it functions both now and in the age to come. The *charismata* are relevant only to this age.

cease/be stilled/pass away ... One day, when God comes again in fullness, prophecy will be fulfilled (and so cease); the indirect communication with God via tongues will no longer be needed (so they are stilled); and since all will be revealed and evident, secret knowledge about God will be redundant (and so pass away). Each of these are partial revelations about God, vital in this present age but unnecessary in the age to come.

v. 11 ... The contrast is between this age (when we are all still children) and the age to come (where we are fulfilled).

v. 12 **Now/then** ... Paul is thinking of the Second Coming; the flowering of the New Age in fullness when God reveals himself, in contrast to the here and now—when, although the New Age has been initiated, it is still incomplete.

poor reflection ... Corinth was famous for the mirrors it made out of highly polished metal. Still, no mirror manufactured in the first century was without imperfections. All of them distorted the image somewhat; and so this is an apt metaphor for the present knowledge of God: it is marred.

v. 13 **remain** ... Charismatic gifts will cease because they brought only partial knowledge of God but three things will carry over into the New Age: faith, hope and love.

A Love Song Is....
by Lewis B. Smedes

A GREAT LOVE SONG is a moment of ecstasy frozen into words, a rhapsody of enthusiasm and passion, a metaphor pointing to a moment when the poet was lifted outside of himself to see reality in its ideal form. It charms us with a memory of the ecstatic moment or allures us with the hint that such a moment might yet be possible. A love song is meant to seduce us from routine into a fantasized ideal of perfect love.

God's love song is in many ways like other great love songs. Its human writer St. Paul was taken outside of himself and his ordinary level of experience and given a vision of ideal love. He saw beyond the normal range of human vision, beyond life's patchwork of routine demands and conflicts, into love's ideal form. He crystallized the qualities of love into simple absolutes that have never—save once—taken solid hold in the network of demands that we recognize as our world. And yet his love song seems somehow meant for our living it. It draws a profile of ideal love, but it is too plain for mystic passion. Love is not jealous, does not get angry quickly, endures very much—these are qualities for ordinary living in ordinary days. This is our challenge: to find ways to bring the heavenly rhapsody down into our own worldly realities.

We are not village saints with little to do but find ways to be nice to needy people. We are salesmen trying to survive for our families' sakes against tough competitors. We are directors of business, who know from experience that "love" is not a byword in the board room. We are union stewards in conflict with an obtuse management. We are husbands and wives trying to survive in a marriage where love has wilted into the boredom of mutual toleration. And we are complicated individuals. We have needs, drives, rights, and goals that do not easily harmonize with self-giving love. Love may be simple. Life is complicated.—*Love Within Limits: A Realist's View of 1 Corinthians 13* (Grand Rapids, MI: Wm. B. Eerdman's Pub. Co., 1978), pp. xi-xii.

UNIT 22—Gifts of Prophecy and Tongues/1 Corinthians 14:1-25

TEXT

Gifts of Prophecy and Tongues

14 Follow the way of love and eagerly desire spiritual gifts, especially the gift of prophecy. ²For anyone who speaks in a tongue does not speak to men but to God. Indeed, no one understands him; he utters mysteries with his spirit. ³But everyone who prophesies speaks to men for their strengthening, encouragement and comfort. ⁴He who speaks in a tongue edifies himself, but he who prophesies edifies the church. ⁵I would like every one of you to speak in tongues, but I would rather have you prophesy. He who prophesies is greater than one who speaks in tongues, unless he interprets, so that the church may be edified.

⁶Now, brothers, if I come to you and speak in tongues, what good will I be to you, unless I bring you some revelation or knowledge or prophecy or word of instruction? ⁷Even in the case of lifeless things that make sounds, such as the flute or harp, how will anyone know what tune is being played unless there is a distinction in the notes? ⁸Again, if the trumpet does not sound a clear call, who will get ready for battle? ⁹So it is with you. Unless you speak intelligible words with your tongue, how will anyone know what you are saying? You will just be speaking into the air. ¹⁰Undoubtedly there are all sorts of languages in the world, yet none of them is without meaning. ¹¹If then I do not grasp the meaning of what someone is saying, I am a foreigner to the speaker, and he is a foreigner to me. ¹²So it is with you. Since you are eager to have spiritual gifts, try to excel in gifts that build up the church.

¹³For this reason the man who speaks in a tongue should pray that he may interpret what he says. ¹⁴For if I pray in a tongue, my spirit prays, but my mind is unfruitful. ¹⁵So what shall I do? I will pray with my spirit, but I will also pray with my mind; I will sing with my spirit, but I will

Continued on next page

STUDY

READ

First Reading/First Impressions
What are a couple words or phrases that seem especially important here?

Second Reading/Big Idea
What is Paul's main point in this passage?

SEARCH

1. How does chapter 14 link back to chapter 12? (see 14:1 and 12:31)

2. What are the three commands Paul gives in verse 1? Given the Corinthian tendency towards spiritual pride, why are these commands especially important?

3. What is the purpose of Paul's contrast of tongues and prophecy? (vv. 2-5)

4. What are two values of each gift? (vv. 2-5)

5. What is Paul's main point in verses 6-12?

6. What three illustrations does he give to illustrate this point? What is the point of each illustration? (vv. 7-8, 10-11)

7. What are the values and limits of the gift of tongues? (vv. 13-19)

8. In what way is their obsession with tongues another mark of their spiritual immaturity? (v. 20; see also 3:1-4)

9. Besides building up the church, what evangelistic purpose do the understandable gifts (like prophecy) serve which tongues does not? (vv. 21-25; also see notes)

APPLY

Those things that seemed flashy, exciting, and powerful were what attracted the Corinthians (this was true in their preference for leaders too—see Paul's ironic comments in 2 Corinthians 11:18-20). In what ways do you see that tendency in yourself? Your church? (Example: "That beautiful singer is more important than I am.")

In the context of your spiritual gifts, what is one way you want to "follow the way of love" this week?

GROUP AGENDA

Divide into groups of 4 before you start to share. And follow the time recommendations.

TO BEGIN/10 Minutes (Choose 1 or 2)
☐ If you could play a musical instrument, what
Continued on next page

---

also sing with my mind. [16]If you are praising God with your spirit, how can one who finds himself among those who do not understand say "Amen" to your thanksgiving, since he does not know what you are saying? [17]You may be giving thanks well enough, but the other man is not edified.

[18]I thank God that I speak in tongues more than all of you. [19]But in the church I would rather speak five intelligible words to instruct others than ten thousand words in a tongue.

[20]Brothers, stop thinking like children. In regard to evil be infants, but in your thinking be adults. [21]In the Law it is written:

"Through men of strange tongues
   and through the lips of foreigners
I will speak to this people,
   but even then they will not listen to me,"
says the Lord.

[22]Tongues, then, are a sign, not for believers but for unbelievers; prophecy, however, is for believers, not for unbelievers. [23]So if the whole church comes together and everyone speaks in tongues, and some who do not understand or some unbelievers come in, will they not say that you are out of your mind? [24]But if an unbeliever or someone who does not understand comes in while everybody is prophesying, he will be convinced by all that he is a sinner and will be judged by all, [25]and the secrets of his heart will be laid bare. So he will fall down and worship God, exclaiming, "God is really among you!"

[a]2 Or *another language;* also in verses 4, 13, 14, 19, 26 and 27   [b]2 Or *by the Spirit*   [c]5 Or *other languages;* also in verses 6, 18, 22, 23 and 39   [d]16 Or *among the inquirers*
[e]21 Isaiah 28:11, 12; Deut. 28:49   [f]23 Or *some inquirers*
[g]24 Or *or some inquirer*

NOTES ON 1 CORINTHIANS 14:1-25

Summary . . . Paul attacks head on the problem they are experiencing with the gift of tongues: during their worship services far too much time was spent speaking in tongues. The result was that chaos, not order, prevailed. No one was edified because no one knew what was going on! In

GROUP AGENDA continued

instrument would it be? ☐ How would you describe yourself in terms of a musical instrument? Are you more like a trumpet, a violin, a banjo, a washboard, the drums, etc.? How would you describe your spouse or the members of your family in terms of musical instruments? ☐ What foreign language(s) have you studied? ☐ Have you ever visited a country where you didn't understand the language? How did you feel? ☐ What did you jot down after READ?

TO GO DEEPER/20 Minutes (Choose 2 or 3)

☐ Share the results of your Bible study, one person taking questions 1, the next person taking questions 2, etc. ☐ What do you learn from the preceding chapter that would be helpful in putting this chapter in context? ☐ What are some biblical principles in this passage on the use of tongues and prophecy?

TO CLOSE/5-20 Minutes (Choose 1 or 2)

☐ What did you put down for APPLY? ☐ Who is someone you identify with the gift of prophecy? Have you known of someone with the gift of tongues? How did these people contribute to your own spiritual growth? ☐ Would you describe your own Bible study group as balanced between "prayer and praise" and deep Bible study? ☐ What would you recommend for your own Bible study group?

these verses he contrasts gifts that are intelligible (such as prophecy) and which edify the community with gifts that are unintelligible (such as tongues) and which edify only the individual.

v. 1 . . . Paul defines the theme of chapter 14 by means of "3 propositions—imperatives that are to be followed in *this* order: First, 'make love your aim' (RSV); second, in that context, 'eagerly desire spiritual gifts;' and third, in your eager desire for gifts which has love as its aim, 'especially (desire) the gift of prophecy.' The Corinthians had precisely the opposite order in their seeking *the* spiritual gift rather than gifts. And their aim was not love but being 'spiritual' " (Fee).

follow . . . In fact, the word might better be translated "pursue." It is virtually synonymous with the next verb *eagerly desire*.

the way of love . . . As defined in chapter 13. The "way of love" is the primary calling for all Christians and the context within which spiritual gifts are to be used.

eagerly desire . . . In 12:31 Paul told the Corinthians: *eagerly desire* the higher gifts. By the re-use of the phrase here he connects chapter 14 back to chapter 12.

vv. 2-5 . . . By means of a series of nicely balanced contrasts, Paul shows why prophecy is to be preferred over tongues.

v. 2 . . . Paul's first point about tongues is that while they may be intelligible to God (who, after all, is the source of tongues) they are not intelligible to other people.

v. 3 . . . In contrast, prophecy is intelligible and brings three benefits to the congregation: it builds them up; it encourages; and it comforts.

prophesies . . . The sense is not so much of future prediction as it is of moral exhortation and theological instruction—probably as related to particular problems and issues being faced by the community.

v. 4 . . . In the second contrast Paul points out *who* is edified by each gift: while tongues edify the individual (and there is no hint that this is not of great value), prophecy edifies many (and the way of love would thus give this gift primary emphasis).

v. 5 . . . While affirming the value of both tongues and prophecy, Paul stresses prophecy because of its value during the worship service.

tongues . . . In verses 2-5 Paul gives insight into just what tongues are. They seem to be a gift from the Holy Spirit whereby an individual "utters mysteries" to God by or in the Spirit; from which great, personal benefit is gained. Uninterpreted tongues, however, are meant to be part of private devotions, not public worship.

greater . . . In the sense that prophecy edifies and is therefore an act of love. Interpreted tongues have the same use and value as prophecy.

vv. 6-12 . . . Now the real issue comes out: intelligibility (v. 9). It appears that it is not just prophecy that Paul is commending (v. 6). Prophecy is just the example he has chosen of an intelligible gift. Here Paul examines the value of various gifts from the point of view of the other people in church.

v. 6 ... The four gifts listed all deal with forms of Christian instruction. It is difficult to distinguish sharply between them. The differences may be in the content of the instruction—*revelation* dealing with hidden aspects of God's truth (Romans 16:25; 2 Corinthians 12:1, 7); *knowledge* as exposition of revealed truth; *prophecy* as insight from God into a specific situation; and a *word of instruction* (literally *teaching*) as the general application of Christian truth.

v. 7 ... He uses musical instruments to illustrate the need for intelligibility. The point of playing them is not just to make sounds but to play a recognizable tune.

v. 8 ... A trumpet can be used to alert an army for battle, but if the wrong note (or a weak note) is sounded, the soldiers will be unclear as to what is expected of them. It will be just noise to them.

v. 9 **speaking into the air** ... This is what tongues are from the standpoint of the hearer—mere random sound.

vv. 10-11 ... The final illustration relates to language. While each language has meaning (tongues presumably have meaning to God), this language, when spoken to a foreigner is just gibberish and one might as well have said nothing.

v. 11 **foreigner** ... The Greek word is *barbaros* (barbarian). Foreigners were so named because to cultured Greek ears their languages sounded like mere gibberish, as if they were saying "brrbrr."

v. 12 ... Paul sums up his argument to this point.

v. 13 **For this reason** ... Because intelligible gifts edify, Paul next shows how tongues might become such.

v. 14-17 ... Paul explains how he understands tongues.

v. 14 **my spirit** ... The work of the Holy Spirit in each Christian is expressed via spiritual gifts; in this case the gift of tongues is in view. Paul both prays and sings in the Spirit in tongues as well as in normal language (in his case, Greek).

v. 15 **pray with my spirit** ... Paul adds another insight into tongues: this is prayer that bypasses the mind. It is, according to verse 15, one quite legitimate (and edifying, v. 4) means of prayer, but it is meant to be complemented with prayer that engages the mind.

v. 16 **those who do not understand** ... This probably refers to other Christians who do not understand tongues. This same Greek word (translated by the above English phrase) is used in verses 23-24 probably to refer to outsiders, perhaps even inquirers (i.e., interested non-Christians).

"**Amen**" ... If a person does not understand what is being said in prayer, it is not possible to offer this traditional response (used in both Jewish and Christian services).

vv. 18-19 ... Paul picks up his argument again and reasserts his view that while tongues are indeed a gift of God ("I thank God that I speak in tongues"), intelligible gifts are to be used in church.

v. 21 ... Paul points to the Old Testament to demonstrate that people will not respond (in repentance and faith) to strange tongues.

v. 22 **tongues, then, are a sign** ... This is a difficult verse, but Paul seems to mean that tongues are a sign of *judgment* against the unbeliever. This is the meaning of the Isaiah text he has just quoted. Likewise, prophecy is a sign of judgment for believers. The Corinthians, however, seem to have closed their ears to faults pointed out via prophecy (which may be another reason why they prefer tongues).

vv. 23-25 ... Paul shifts back to his original line of reasoning, but this time he contrasts the negative impact of tongues with the positive impact of prophecy *on unbelievers*. Prior to this Paul has been concerned about the impact of tongues and prophecy on *believers*.

everyone speaks in tongues ... The Corinthian worship service must have been a cacophony of noise and confusion (at times) with the simultaneous exercise of the gift of tongues (see also v. 27).

v. 23 **out of your mind** ... Not in the modern sense of "insane" but in the ancient sense of "possessed by a spirit."

v. 25 ... Prophecy evokes conviction and commitment; tongues evoke nothing more than a cognitive sense that the speaker is possessed in the same way as devotees from other religions.

fall down ... And thus acknowledge his/her own unworthiness before God.

UNIT 23—Orderly Worship/1 Corinthians 14:26-39

TEXT

Orderly Worship

26What then shall we say, brothers? When you come together, everyone has a hymn, or a word of instruction, a revelation, a tongue or an interpretation. All of these must be done for the strengthening of the church. 27If anyone speaks in a tongue, two—or at the most three—should speak, one at a time, and someone must interpret. 28If there is no interpreter, the speaker should keep quiet in the church and speak to himself and God.

29Two or three prophets should speak, and the others should weigh carefully what is said. 30And if a revelation comes to someone who is sitting down, the first speaker should stop. 31For you can all prophesy in turn so that everyone may be instructed and encouraged. 32The spirits of prophets are subject to the control of prophets. 33For God is not a God of disorder but of peace.

As in all the congregations of the saints, 34women should remain silent in the churches. They are not allowed to speak, but must be in submission, as the Law says. 35If they want to inquire about something, they should ask their own husbands at home; for it is disgraceful for a woman to speak in the church. 36Did the word of God originate with you? Or are you the only people it has reached?

37If anybody thinks he is a prophet or spiritually gifted, let him acknowledge that what I am writing to you is the Lord's command. 38If he ignores this, he himself will be ignored.

39Therefore, my brothers, be eager to prophesy, and do not forbid speaking in tongues. 40But everything should be done in a fitting and orderly way.

a38 Some manuscripts this, let him ignore this

STUDY

READ

First Reading/First Impressions
What would you suggest as a creative title for this section?

Second Reading/Big Idea
What verse is the key to this passage?

SEARCH

1. Given the need for Paul's instructions about public worship, describe the sights, sounds, and feelings going on in a Corinthian worship service beforehand.

2. Using the information here, what should their services be like?

3. In light of his statement about God in verse 33, what is the purpose of his directives about tongues and prophecy in verses 27-32?

4. Paraphrase the principles he gives for public worship in verses 26b, 33, and 40.

(26b)

(33)

(40)

5. In light of 11:5, verses 34-36 are difficult to understand (see notes). What type of talk, contributing to the general disorder of their services, might be in view here?

APPLY

Although Paul wanted to tone down the atmosphere of the Corinthian worship services which were too much like the frenzied, ecstatic services at the pagan temples, what positive qualities about public worship might you and your church learn from the extremism of the Corinthians?

(Example: we ought to encourage a more widespread participation of people)

The New Testament does not give a blueprint for the conduct of public worship, but the principles of strengthening one another, representing the peace of God, and propriety can take different forms in different times and cultures. Yet, since many of our churches practice traditions that are more reflective of an earlier culture (such as incense, formal language, organ music, etc.), newcomers today often feel very awkward. In light of our culture, what is one way public worship services might help newcomers feel the peace of God rather than feeling strange and out of place?

Likewise, what is one idea for how public worship might better strengthen the members?

GROUP AGENDA

Divide into groups of 4 before you start to share. And follow the time recommendations.

TO BEGIN/10 Minutes (Choose 1 or 2)

☐ What is one of your favorite hymns or Christian choruses? What is the chorus or hymn you associate with your childhood?
☐ How big a part does music play in your life now? What is your favorite kind of music?
☐ What is one of the best worship services you ever attended? What made this service so special? ☐ What did you jot down for READ?

TO GO DEEPER/20 Minutes (Choose 2 or 3)

☐ Go around and share what you noted in the SEARCH portion of the Bible study, one question at a time. ☐ How would you compare the order of service in your own church to the directives given in this passage? ☐ How do you harmonize Paul's teaching about women in verses 34-36, with his teaching elsewhere on the equality of all believers in Christ? ☐ Case History: Your church tends to lose young people when they leave for college. It's not that they give up their faith, for many become more involved and committed to Christ than ever. But they gravitate towards informal fellowships in homes and small groups rather than identifying with the church. What are some signals you ought to be picking up that might help your church better serve young people in general?

TO CLOSE/5-20 Minutes (Choose 1 or 2)

☐ What did you put down for APPLY in the study? ☐ What is the closest you have come to sharing in a fellowship like the fellowship described in verses 26-33? What would you like to bring from that experience to your church today? ☐ What is one wish you have for your church? For your Bible study group?

NOTES ON 1 CORINTHIANS 14:26-39

Summary . . . Paul concludes this major section (begun in 11:2) by outlining quite specifically how certain spiritual gifts are to be used when the church assembles together—his main point being that when it comes to worship, order not disorder is the way of God.

v. 26 . . . Paul reiterates that *each* believer has a gift to offer during worship; that there is a variety of gifts; and that gifts are to be used to edify.

a hymn . . . Singing is a gift. The reference here may be to "singing in the Spirit" (v. 15).

all of these . . . Probably a representative list of the sort of gifts used during worship. The list is not exhaustive because it does not include, for example, prophecy or discernment of spirits, previously mentioned in the context of worship and assumed in the verses that follow.

vv. 27-28 . . . Paul offers guidelines for the use of tongues—only two or three are to speak; one at a time; and never (in church) without interpretation.

vv. 29-33 . . . Here he gives guidelines for prophecy: two or three speak followed by discernment.

v. 29 **weigh carefully** . . . Simply because a prophecy is uttered does not make it automatically true. Not only does its "source" have to be noted by those gifted in such discernment (12:10) but its content must be considered carefully by the whole assembled body (12:3; 1 Thessalonians 5:20-21).

vv. 31-32 . . . These "seem to be directives against those who would tend to dominate and talk too long" (Fee).

v. 31 . . . While it is true that certain individuals held the office of prophet (and had a special, recognized gift of prophecy; Acts 11:27-28, 21:9-11); here Paul says that on occasion anyone might exercise the gift of prophecy (including women; 11:5).

v. 32 . . . In fact, a prophet can control his/her utterance. A prophet is not gripped in such a frenzy that "automatic speaking" results which bypasses the control of the person. Thus order is possible within the assembly.

v. 33b . . . It can be argued that the last half of verse 33 belongs not with verse 34 as the NIV has it but with the first half of verse 33. (The way the NIV translates this, the phrase "in all the congregations" is followed awkwardly by the parallel phrase in verse 34 "in the churches."). In other words, Paul is saying that God is the God of peace in *all* congregations.

vv. 34-35 . . . These are very difficult verses to interpret since they seem to contradict chapter 11 (especially 11:5), where Paul indicates that as long as women are suitably clothed they can pray and prophesy during public worship. A variety of solutions have been proposed: (a) that verses 34-35 were a later addition to the text, not by Paul (v. 33 flows smoothly into v. 36); (b) that what Paul prohibits is women passing judgment on prophecy as in verse 29; (c) that the reference is to uninspired "chatter" (the word means this in classical Greek) by the women which is adding to the chaos. Obviously Paul understood how verses 34-35 fitted with 11:2-16, since he would not have written contradictory advice. The problem is that no one today knows for sure what is meant.

v. 36 . . . Now Paul concludes by directly confronting the Corinthians over the fact that they considered "tongues" as that which made one "spiritual." In this matter, they cannot assume that they alone know the truth nor that God gave only them this insight.

vv. 37-38 . . . As to those who are teaching this, if they are really inspired by the Holy Spirit as Paul indeed knows that he is (2:16; 7:40) they cannot help but agree. The Spirit does not inspire opposing messages.

vv. 39-40 . . . Paul summarizes chapter 14 with three commands; the first two relate to verses 1-25 and the third to verses 26-35.

COMMENTS

Tongues and Interpretation

by Peter Wagner

The gift of tongues is the special ability that God gives to certain members of the Body of Christ (A) to speak to God in a language they have never learned and/or (B) to receive and communicate an immediate message of God to His people through a divinely-anointed utterance in a language they have never learned....

Private tongues are often referred to as "Prayer language." No accompanying gift of interpretation is involved. The biblical text most descriptive of this is 1 Corinthians 14:28 where Paul says that tongues without interpretation should not be used in the church, but rather the person who has such a gift should "speak to himself, and to God." Since this is highly experiential, I am going to describe it by using the experiences of a Christian brother.

Robert Tuttle is an esteemed colleague of mine on the faculty of Fuller Seminary and a United Methodist minister. His gift is private tongues. He says, "There are times in my devotional life when I can no longer find words to express my 'innards.' ... At that point I allow the Holy Spirit to pray through me in a language that I did not learn. Believe me, I know what it means to learn a language. I struggle with the biblical languages every day ... I say a language because I believe it to be a language. My vocabulary is growing. I know enough about language to be able to identify sentence structure. My unknown tongue or prayer language has periods, commas, and exclamation points. It is a marvelous gift."

Not all students of spiritual gifts agree that this is a real language. Some professional linguists have tape-recorded persons speaking in tongues and said they find no linguistic structure. But since they haven't taped all tongues, maybe the ones they did tape were so-called ecstatic utterances while others, like Tuttle's, may be languages. In any case, I find the point too academic because whether ecstatic utterances or structure languages, the function is the same. This function has been described by Harald Bredesen, pastor of North County Christian Center in San Marcos, California, in several postulates:

1. "Tongues enable our spirits to communicate directly with God above and beyond the power of our minds to understand."

2. "Tongues liberate the Spirit of God within us."

3. "Tongues enable the spirit to take its place of ascendancy over soul and body."

4. "Tongues are God's provision for catharsis, therefore important to our mental health."

5. "Tongues meet our needs for a whole new language for worship, prayer and praise."

Part B or public tongues is intimately related to the gift of interpretation. Without interpretation the gift is useless and has no part in the church (see 1 Corinthians 14:27, 28).

The gift of interpretation is the special ability that God gives to certain members of the Body of Christ to make known in the vernacular the message of one who speaks in tongues.

Quite often, but not always, tongues-interpretation functions as a hyphenated gift. Michael Green says, "Though some men have the gift of interpretation who cannot themselves speak in tongues, this is unusual; for the most part it is those who already have tongues who gain this further gift of interpretation." This means that some people give messages in public in tongues and immediately interpret what they themselves have said. In other cases one will give the message and another will interpret.

By way of example I will relate a secondhand anecdote that I received from a very reliable source. It involves a group of believers in a remote Guatemalan village. A severe drought had devastated the area and the village was on the verge of extinction. The Christians prayed and God spoke to the group through a message in tongues. He told them to go up on a hill which was owned by the Christians and dig a well. It seemed to be one of the most illogical places to do it, but they obeyed, even in the face of the ridicule of the unbelievers in the village. The ridicule changed to astonishment, however, when they soon struck an abundant supply of water and the entire village was saved. Many unbelievers also were saved when they saw the power of God. Maybe this is what Paul had in mind when he wrote, "Tongues are for a sign, not to them that believe, but to them that believe not" (1 Corinthians 14:22).—Taken from *Your Spiritual Gifts Can Help Your Church Grow* (Regal Books), pp. 233-236.

UNIT 24—The Resurrection of Christ/1 Corinthians 15:1-11

TEXT

The Resurrection of Christ

15 Now, brothers, I want to remind you of the gospel I preached to you, which you received and on which you have taken your stand. ²By this gospel you are saved, if you hold firmly to the word I preached to you. Otherwise, you have believed in vain.

³For what I received I passed on to you as of first importance: that Christ died for our sins according to the Scriptures, ⁴that he was buried, that he was raised on the third day according to the Scriptures, ⁵and that he appeared to Peter,ᵇ and then to the Twelve. ⁶After that, he appeared to more than five hundred of the brothers at the same time, most of whom are still living, though some have fallen asleep. ⁷Then he appeared to James, then to all the apostles, ⁸and last of all he appeared to me also, as to one abnormally born.

⁹For I am the least of the apostles and do not even deserve to be called an apostle, because I persecuted the church of God. ¹⁰But by the grace of God I am what I am, and his grace to me was not without effect. No, I worked harder than all of them—yet not I, but the grace of God that was with me. ¹¹Whether, then, it was I or they, this is what we preach, and this is what you believed.

ᵃ3 Or *you at the first*   ᵇ5 Greek *Cephas*

STUDY

READ

First Reading/First Impressions
What is Paul doing here? ☐ Giving them the "bottom line" on Christianity? ☐ Saying, "If you don't believe me, check it out." ☐ Reminding them of a basic truth they were slipping away from.

Second Reading/Big Idea
What do you see as two main points in this passage?

SEARCH

1. What might be happening in the church that Paul would consider it important to remind them of the gospel? (vv. 1-2)

2. What facts about Christ are of "first importance" in Paul's presentation of the gospel? (vv. 3-8)

3. What parallels do you see between these facts and Paul's first recorded sermon in Acts 13:23-39?

4. What reasons may lie behind Paul's emphasis on Christ's appearances? (vv. 5-8)

104

5. Specifically, why would he emphasize Christ's appearance to himself? (v. 8)

6. What is Paul's point in verse 9-10?

7. How does Paul's past (v. 9—see Acts 9:1-2) account for his patience with the problems of this church?

APPLY

Christ's death and resurrection stand as the two central themes of the apostle's preaching in Acts, as well as the central realities of our faith to which Paul and the other New Testament writers continually refer. In your own words, write out what you understand as some of the meaning and implications behind the reality of his death and his resurrection. Feel free to refer to other passages for help.

His death means . . .

His resurrection means . . .

GROUP AGENDA

Divide into groups of 4 before you start to share. And follow the time recommendations.

TO BEGIN / 10 Minutes (Choose 1 or 2)

☐ "If I've told you once, I've told you a thousand times . . ." Over what issue was that true of your parents with you? Of you with your kids? ☐ Are you more like a "Gullible George" or a "Sally Skeptic"? Why? ☐ What did you write for READ? ☐ What is one saying or lesson your parents taught you that has really proved to be helpful to you?

TO GO DEEPER / 20 Minutes (Choose 2 or 3)

☐ Go around and share the SEARCH part of the Bible study. ☐ If you had to boil down the Christian religion to the historical facts, would you add anything else to what Paul says here? Why? ☐ Why do you think Paul had to forcefully underscore these historical facts to the Corinthians? ☐ What is the latest "heresy" you have heard about the resurrection of Jesus and how would this passage answer it? ☐ Case History: Johnny grew up in a Christian home where he accepted the historical facts of Jesus as true. In college, however, he was confronted with some professors who challenged his naivete, and he became an agnostic. Johnny, in turn, accuses you of "leaving your brains at the church door." What is your response?

TO CLOSE / 5-20 Minutes (Choose 1 or 2)

☐ What did you put down for APPLY? ☐ When, if ever, did you question the historical facts of the gospel? Where are you right now? ☐ How effective are you at passing on your faith? What have you found is the best way for you to share your faith? ☐ For a person who finds it difficult to accept the historical facts of the gospel, what have you found is the best approach in sharing your faith with this person?

NOTES ON 1 CORINTHIANS 15:1-11

Section Summary/1 Corinthians 15 ... Paul now turns to a *theological* problem in contrast to the largely behavioral problems he has dealt with thus far. Some Corinthians are denying that in the future believers will be raised from the dead. The problem may be simply one of ignorance. No one ever instructed them in this matter. (The Thessalonians, for example, did not know about the resurrection of the dead as Paul says in 1 Thessalonians 4:13-18). Furthermore, the Corinthians might have resisted this concept since it ran counter to the gnostic idea that death released the spirit to return to God and the useless body (in the gnostic view) fell away like a discarded husk. Or like Hymenaeus and Philetus, they might have "spiritualized" the resurrection, saying that it has already taken place (2 Timothy 2:17-18).

Unit Summary/1 Corinthians 15:1-11 ... Paul begins by pointing to something the Corinthians believed: that Christ rose from the dead. Christ's resurrection is the key to Paul's argument that believers will also be resurrected.

v. 1 **gospel** ... Literally "good news," a term used in Greek literature to signify a positive event of great significance; as for example, the birth of a future emperor or the winning of an important battle; used by Paul (and others in the New Testament) to designate the core message of Christianity, that in Jesus Christ, God fulfilled his promises and opened a way of salvation to all people. In the next few verses Paul will define the content of this message.

v. 2 ... It is as a result of belief (trust) in the good news of Christ's death and resurrection that salvation comes.

vv. 3-4 ... This is the earliest written definition of the "gospel." It consists of three statements of historical fact: Christ died, was buried, and rose again; and two words of explanation: he died "for our sins" (i.e., to deal with them) and all this is "according to Scripture" (i.e., a fulfillment of God's plan).

v. 3 **what I received** ... Paul did not make up the gospel. It was common to the church. He simply passed on what he had been given.

for our sins ... When Christ died, it was in order to deal with the fact of our sin. By his death in our place as our substitute, Christ enabled men and women to be forgiven for their sins; to come back into relationship with God; and to have new life.

according to the Scriptures ... Christ's death fulfilled the prophecies found in Old Testament Scripture (e.g., Isaiah 52:13-53:12). "This means that it was not fortuitous, but willed and determined by God, and that it formed part of the winding up of his eternal purpose; that is, that it was one of those eschatological events that stand on the frontier between the present age and the age to come, in which the divine purpose reaches its completion" (Barrett).

v. 4 **he was buried** ... i.e., he was really dead; and so he really rose from the dead. It was a real resurrection not just resuscitation.

he was raised ... Paul shifts the tense of the verb (in Greek) from the aorist tense (completed past action)—"died/buried" to the perfect tense with the idea that what once happened is even now still in force. "Christ died, but he is not dead; he was buried, but he is not in the grave; he was raised, and he is alive now" (Barrett).

vv. 5-8 **appeared** ... Paul's emphasis in this statement of the gospel is on the resurrection (because of the argument he is building in chapter 15) so here he points to six post-resurrection appearances, each of which substantiate that Christ indeed rose.

v. 5 **he appeared to Peter** ... Luke 24:34 and Mark 16:7.

the Twelve ... Matthew 28:16-20; Luke 24:31-51; John 20:19-23.

v. 6 **most of whom are still living** ... Paul is inviting people to check out for themselves the reality of the resurrection. What he is saying is: "There are nearly 500 people who some 20 years ago saw Jesus after his resurrection. Ask one of them." This is a strong proof of the resurrection because in this public letter Paul would never have challenged people in this way if these witnesses had not, indeed, seen the resurrected Christ and could therefore be counted upon to verify this fact.

vv. 9-11 ... For the third time (chapters 1-4; chapter 9) Paul defends his apostleship. Having used his own experience of the resurrected Lord as one of his six examples, it is quite natural to use it also to demonstrate the fact of his apostleship.

v. 11 ... Paul reiterates once more that the gospel he has just described is common to the church; preached by all; and believed by the Corinthians.

COMMENTS

The Significance of the Resurrection
by John R. W. Stott

Clearly the resurrection has great significance. If it can be shown that Jesus of Nazareth rose from the dead, it is beyond dispute that He was a unique figure. It is not a question of his spiritual survival, nor of his physical resuscitation, but of his conquest of death and his resurrection to a new plane of existence altogether. We do not know of anyone else who has had this experience....

We may not feel that His resurrection establishes His deity conclusively, but we must agree that it is suggestive of it. It is fitting that a supernatural person should enter and leave the earth in a supernatural way. This is in fact what the New Testament teaches and the Church believes. His birth was natural, but his conception was supernatural. His death was natural, but his resurrection was supernatural. His miraculous conception and resurrection do not prove his deity, but they are congruous with it. We are not concerned here with his so-called "Virgin Birth." There is good reason to believe it, but it is not used in the New Testament to prove him Messiah and Son of God, as is the resurrection. Jesus himself never predicted his passion without adding that He would rise, and described his coming resurrection as a "sign." St. Paul, at the beginning of his Epistle to the Romans, writes that Jesus was "designated Son of God in power ... by his resurrection from the dead" (i.4), and the earliest sermons of the apostles recorded in the Acts repeatedly assert that by the resurrection God has reversed man's sentence and vindicated his Son.

Of this resurrection St. Luke, who is known to have been an accurate and painstaking historian, says there are "many infallible proofs" (Acts 1:3 AV). We may not feel able to go as far as Matthew Arnold who called the resurrection "the best attested fact in history," but certainly many impartial students have judged the evidence to be extremely good. For instance, Sir Edward Clarke, K.C., wrote to the Rev. E. L. Macassey, D.D.: "As a lawyer I have made a prolonged study of the evidences for the events of the first Easter Day. To me the evidence is conclusive, and over and over again in the High Court I have secured the verdict on evidence not nearly so compelling. Inference follows on evidence, and a truthful witness is always artless and disdains effect. The Gospel evidence for the resurrection is of this class, and as a lawyer I accept it unreservedly as the testimony of truthful men to facts they were able to substantiate."—*Basic Christianity* (Grand Rapids, MI: Wm. B. Eerdmans, 1958) pp. 45-46.

Explaining the Resurrection
by John Warwick Montgomery

Of course, attempts have been made to "explain" the resurrection accounts naturalistically. The German rationalist Venturini suggested that Jesus only fainted on the cross and subsequently revived in the cool tomb. This "swoon theory" is typical of all such arguments: They are infinitely more improbable than the resurrection itself, and they fly squarely in the face of the documentary evidence. Jesus surely died on the cross, for Roman crucifixion teams knew their business (they had enough practice). He could not possibly have rolled the heavy boulder from the door of the tomb after the crucifixion experience.

And even if we discounted these impossibilities, what happened to him later? If we agree that he died and was interred, then the explanation that the body was stolen is no more helpful. For who would have taken it? Surely not the Romans or the Jewish parties, for they wished at all costs to squelch the Christian sect. And certainly not the Christians, for to do so and then fabricate detailed accounts of Jesus' resurrection would have been to fly in the face of the ethic their master preached and for which they ultimately died....

Note that when the disciples of Jesus proclaimed the resurrection, they did so as eyewitnesses and they did so while people were still alive who had had contact with the events they spoke of. In A.D. 56, Paul wrote that over 500 people had seen the risen Jesus and that most of them were still alive (1 Cor. 15:1ff). It passes the bounds of credibility that the early Christians could have manufactured such a tale and then preached it among those who might easily have refuted it simply by producing the body of Jesus—*History and Christianity* (Downers Grove, IL: InterVarsity Press 1964) pp. 76-78.

UNIT 25—The Resurrection of the Dead/1 Corinthians 15:12-34

TEXT

The Resurrection of the Dead

¹²But if it is preached that Christ has been raised from the dead, how can some of you say that there is no resurrection of the dead? ¹³If there is no resurrection of the dead, then not even Christ has been raised. ¹⁴And if Christ has not been raised, our preaching is useless and so is your faith. ¹⁵More than that, we are then found to be false witnesses about God, for we have testified about God that he raised Christ from the dead. But he did not raise him if in fact the dead are not raised. ¹⁶For if the dead are not raised, then Christ has not been raised either. ¹⁷And if Christ has not been raised, your faith is futile; you are still in your sins. ¹⁸Then those also who have fallen asleep in Christ are lost. ¹⁹If only for this life we have hope in Christ, we are to be pitied more than all men.

²⁰But Christ has indeed been raised from the dead, the firstfruits of those who have fallen asleep. ²¹For since death came through a man, the resurrection of the dead comes also through a man. ²²For as in Adam all die, so in Christ all will be made alive. ²³But each in his own turn: Christ, the firstfruits; then, when he comes, those who belong to him. ²⁴Then the end will come, when he hands over the kingdom to God the Father after he has destroyed all dominion, authority and power. ²⁵For he must reign until he has put all his enemies under his feet. ²⁶The last enemy to be destroyed is death. ²⁷For he "has put everything under his feet." Now when it says that "everything" has been put under him, it is clear that this does not include God himself, who put everything under Christ. ²⁸When he has done this, then the Son himself will be made subject to him who put everything under him, so that God may be all in all.

²⁹Now if there is no resurrection, what will those do who are baptized for the dead? If the dead are not raised at all, why are people

Continued on next page

STUDY

READ

First Reading/First Impressions

My feeling about this passage is that it . . . ☐ deals with things I already know about. ☐ highlights the importance of Christ's resurrection for all the Christian life. ☐ deals with a grave error in this church.

Second Reading/Big Idea

In a sentence or two, what is Paul's big concern here?

SEARCH

1. What false doctrine is being taught in the Corinthian church? (v. 12—see notes)

2. Locate the 11 "ifs" in verses 12-19 and 29-34. Now identify the 11 conclusions which would be true if there was no resurrection.

3. What is the central proof Paul continually points to as evidence for the hope of our resurrection?

4. What does the idea of the "first fruits" (vv. 20, 23) show about how Christ's resurrection relates to ours?

5. What analogy does he use in verses 21-22?

6. The resurrection of the believers will be part of what great event? How will the events unfold? List the events in sequence. (vv. 23-28)

7. What problems emerge both for the Corinthians and Paul if there is no resurrection? (vv. 29-34)

APPLY

If an agnostic who did not know what he believed about the resurrection of Jesus Christ from the dead asked you to defend your position, what reasons would you give for your belief?

First, read Matthew 28, Mark 16, Luke 24 and John 20-21. Then, list five historical facts from these passages to justify your position on Jesus' resurrection from the dead.

FIVE REASONS I BELIEVE THAT JESUS ROSE FROM THE DEAD   CROSS REFERENCES

1 _____ _____

2 _____ _____

3 _____ _____

4 _____ _____

5 _____ _____

GROUP AGENDA

Divide into groups of 4 before you start to share. And follow the time recommendations.

TO BEGIN/10 Minutes (Choose 1 or 2)

☐ What is one of the most beautiful and meaningful funeral services you ever attended? ☐ If you had to choose the music for your funeral right now, what would you choose? Why? ☐ If you could write an epitaph or inscription for your tombstone, what would you put on it? ☐ What did you put down for READ?

TO GO DEEPER/20 Minutes (Choose 2 or 3)

☐ What did you put down under SEARCH in the Bible study? ☐ What is the connection between the historical fact of the resurrection of Christ and the believer's hope in his/her own after-life? ☐ In contrast to the Epicurean philosophy of life described in verse 32, what is the believer's philosophy of life? How does the Christian philosophy of life provide solace and consolation in times of pain, suffering and death? ☐ Case History: Cancer has taken the

Continued on next page

---

baptized for them? [30]And as for us, why do we endanger ourselves every hour? [31]I die every day—I mean that, brothers—just as surely as I glory over you in Christ Jesus our Lord. [32]If I fought wild beasts in Ephesus for merely human reasons, what have I gained? If the dead are not raised,

"Let us eat and drink,
for tomorrow we die."

[33]Do not be misled: "Bad company corrupts good character." [34]Come back to your senses as you ought, and stop sinning; for there are some who are ignorant of God—I say this to your shame.

[a]27 Psalm 8:6   [b]32 Isaiah 22:13

NOTES ON 1 CORINTHIANS 15:12-34

Summary ... By means of a series of "if ... then" arguments Paul shows that to deny the future resurrection of believers one must also deny the past resurrection of Jesus, which in fact they apparently did *not* deny.

v. 12 **But** ... Having established the fact of Christ's own resurrection (vv. 3-8), Paul now pushes the argument forward: Jesus' resurrection is a clear proof that there is such a thing as resurrection.

how can some of you say ... Now Paul pinpoints directly the false teaching against which he is contending.

vv. 13-15 ... In the next if/then argument Paul shows that *if* resurrection is impossible *then:* (a) Christ could not have been raised; (b) Paul's own preaching is without value; (c) their faith is meaningless; and (d) they are lying about God.

v. 14 **our preaching/your faith** ... The Corinthians owe their very existence as a church to these two things: Paul's preaching and their response of faith. Central to both that preaching and their faith is the resurrection of Christ. And since the church does indeed exist (and experiences the power and presence of God) this is another proof of the resurrection.

v. 16 **if the dead are not raised** ... This is the first of three times in this section (vv. 12-34) that Paul uses this phrase by which he summarizes the implications of their errant view about the resurrection of the body. If the dead are not raised then: (a) Christ could not have been resurrected (and they believe that he was); (b) there would be no point in baptizing people for the dead (as they were apparently doing, v. 29); (c) and believers might as well "live it up" since they had no future (v. 32).

vv. 18-19 ... Relentlessly he points out the implications of no resurrection: (a) they are still lost and dead in sin; (b) those who have died are lost; (c) their "hope" is groundless; and (d) they are pitiable people. In other words, without resurrection, Christianity crumbles.

vv. 20-28 ... Paul will now show how future resurrection of believers is the logical outcome of Christ's past resurrection.

v. 20 **But Christ has indeed been raised** ... Having sketched the horror of no resurrection, Paul relieves the gloom and shifts to this positive affirmation of what is indeed so. This is the core affirmation without which there is no Christianity.

first fruits ... Those early developing grains or fruits that demonstrate to the relief and delight of the farmer that indeed the full harvest is not far behind. In the same way the fact that Christ was raised from the dead is clear proof (to the relief and delight of the Christian) that the future resurrection of believers is assured. (See also Romans 8:23, 29; 11:16 for other uses by Paul of the idea of first fruits).

vv. 21-22 ... From the metaphor of the first fruits Paul moves to the analogy of Christ and Adam. It is via Adam that all died. It is via Christ that death is undone. Paul will treat this metaphor in more detail in verses 45-49.

v. 22 **Adam** ... Adam sinned and so death entered into the world (Genesis 2:17) and thus all people since that time experience death (Romans 5:12-21).

all will be made alive ... Though the wording has been made parallel to the previous clause *(all die)* the idea is that all who are *in Christ* will rise, as Paul says explicitly in 1 Thessalonians 4:16.

vv. 23-28 ... Paul returns to the metaphor of the firstfruits, showing how it relates to the Second Coming. In order for the Corinthians to understand the future resurrection, Paul must place it in the context of the Apocalypse—that time when Christ returns and the New Age in its fullness is ushered in.

v. 23 ... Christ was raised on the third day after his death (v. 4). Christians will be raised at his second coming.

v. 24 ... After Christ has defeated the powers of evil, He will hand over the then-secured kingdom to God—the key event of the End Times.

GROUP AGENDA continued

life of your friend and now you are called upon to comfort his children. "Why does a good God let bad things happen," they ask you? What is your response?

TO CLOSE/5-20 Minutes (Choose 1 or 2)

☐ What did you put down for APPLY? ☐ When did you come to the point in your own spiritual understanding that you connected the resurrection of Christ with your own ultimate victory over the grave? ☐ Quite frankly, does the fact that one day you will be raised from the dead to spend eternity with God make a nickel's worth of difference in the way you live today? How? ☐ What is the most significant thing you have learned from this passage?

COMMENTS

v. 25 ... Psalms 110:1.

v. 26 ... The last of these enemies to be rendered impotent (inoperative) is death itself. That Christ has won out is seen in the resurrection of believers.

vv. 27-28 ... Paul explains Psalms 8:6.

vv. 29-34 ... Thus far Paul has shown that there is a resurrection for believers in the future. In this section he strengthens his case by pointing out that both his actions and theirs demonstrate a belief in the resurrection.

v. 29 **if there is no resurrection** ... Here Paul gives the first of three arguments which point out the absurdity of an action if there is no coming resurrection. In verse 29, the absurd action is baptism for the dead; in verses 30-32a it is Paul exposing himself to constant danger; and in verses 32b-34, it is morality in general that would make no sense.

baptized for the dead ... It seems that amongst the many strange things that happened at Corinth was the practice (by some) of vicarious baptism, whereby a living person was immersed in water on behalf of a dead person so as to secure, almost magically, the benefits of baptism for the departed friend. At least this is the best guess of scholars.

vv. 30-32a ... Paul next argues that it is absurd for him to undergo the dangers he does for the sake of Christianity if there is no hope of the resurrection.

v. 32a **fought wild beasts** ... Paul is probably speaking metaphorically. If he had actually survived being thrown to the beasts (as an act of punishment), he would have been deprived of Roman citizenship. From *Acts* it is clear that he still was a citizen well after the time this letter was written. Likewise it is unlikely that such an experience would have been left out of *Acts* or out of his list of dangers in 2 Corinthians 11:23f. This metaphoric use, however, makes the danger and suffering no less real.

vv. 32b-34 ... The third appeal goes like this: *if there is no resurrection, then there is nothing in the future for a person; therefore,* life has no purpose beyond the here and now—so live it up!

v. 33 **"Bad company corrupts good character"** ... This is a quote taken from the comedy *Thais* written by Menander. It had become a well-known proverb by Paul's time. Paul generally quoted from the Old Testament, so this quotation from a secular source is an unusual departure for him.

Baptism for the Dead
by Wayne A. Meeks

We have squeezed about all the information we can from the quotations and allusions in the literature. Yet we surmise that the Pauline Christians used still other ceremonies of which we know virtually nothing. We know, for example, that some of them died during the span of time covered by the letters, and we know that funeral rituals were of enormous importance to people in Greek and Roman society. A great many of the clubs we have mentioned were formed primarily to assure the associates a decent burial and memorial. We can be certain that the congregations Paul founded provided equivalent services for their members, but, apart from one utterly enigmatic remark, the letters say nothing at all about what was done for those who, as they said, "had fallen asleep." Probably the Christians buried their dead in the same places and in the same fashion as their neighbors. Those who could afford it probably erected inscriptions recalling high points of the deceased's life, indicating significant titles of status or profession, and giving the dates—but if they did, either the inscriptions remain lost or there was nothing overtly Christian about them to distinguish them from the others that have been found. The commonest memorial rite was a meal in honor of the departed, often around a table-shaped stone in the cemetery, on several specific anniversaries of the day of death. In later centuries this practice was common among Christians as among pagans—the first clear evidence is in Tertullian. Nothing would seem more natural than for the Christians of Paul's groups, for whom common meals were already so important, to hold funeral meals for deceased brothers as well—either separately, or as part of the Lord's Supper, which was already an *anamnèsis* of the Lord's death. Yet there is not a word about such meals, not even in the consolation that Paul offers the Thessalonian Christians (1 Thessalonians 4:13-18), where we might have expected it. Perhaps the customs were too well known to mention. Paradoxically, the one practice that is mentioned, in 1 Corinthians 15:29, is mystifying to us. Paul is arguing with the *pneumatikoi* at Corinth that resurrection does not mean only spiritual exaltation now, but a real, future resurrection of the dead body. "Otherwise," he asks, "what are they doing who are baptized for the dead? If the dead are not raised at all, why are they baptized on their behalf?" What are they doing? The Corinthians presumably knew, but we do not, despite interesting speculations without end.—Taken from *The First Urban Christians* (Yale Univ. Press), p. 162.

UNIT 26—The Resurrection of the Body/1 Corinthians 15:35-58

TEXT

The Resurrection Body

35But someone may ask, "How are the dead raised? With what kind of body will they come?" 36How foolish! What you sow does not come to life unless it dies. 37When you sow, you do not plant the body that will be, but just a seed, perhaps of wheat or of something else. 38But God gives it a body as he has determined, and to each kind of seed he gives its own body. 39All flesh is not the same: Men have one kind of flesh, animals have another, birds another and fish another. 40There are also heavenly bodies and there are earthly bodies; but the splendor of the heavenly bodies is one kind, and the splendor of the earthly bodies is another. 41The sun has one kind of splendor, the moon another and the stars another; and star differs from star in splendor.

42So will it be with the resurrection of the dead. The body that is sown is perishable, it is raised imperishable; 43it is sown in dishonor, it is raised in glory; it is sown in weakness, it is raised in power; 44it is sown a natural body, it is raised a spiritual body.

If there is a natural body, there is also a spiritual body. 45So it is written: "The first man Adam became a living being"; the last Adam, a life-giving spirit. 46The spiritual did not come first, but the natural, and after that the spiritual. 47The first man was of the dust of the earth, the second man from heaven. 48As was the earthly man, so are those who are of the earth; and as is the man from heaven, so also are those who are of heaven. 49And just as we have borne the likeness of the earthly man, so shall we bear the likeness of the man from heaven.

50I declare to you, brothers, that flesh and blood cannot inherit the kingdom of God, nor does the perishable inherit the imperishable. 51Listen, I tell you a mystery: We will not all sleep, but we will all be changed—52in a flash, in the twinkling of an eye, at the last trumpet.

STUDY

READ

First Reading/First Impressions

If I try to "listen" to what Paul sounds like here, it's like he is . . . ☐ a teacher giving a lecture. ☐ a preacher really caught up in the sermon? ☐ a political leader trying to rouse up the nation. ☐ Other __

Second Reading/Big Idea

What is the most important verse here? Why?

SEARCH

1. What practical problem undercuts belief in the resurrection for some of these people? (v. 35)

2. How does Paul's analogy with the seed deal with this objection? (v. 38)

3. How does the analogy of the different types of bodies relate to the objection? (vv. 39-41)

4. What can you learn about the resurrected body from verses 42-44?

5. What is the point of the comparison between Adam and Christ? (vv. 45-49)

112 *Continued on next page*

6. What are some of the implications you can think of from the truth that "we shall bear the likeness of the man from heaven"? (v. 49)

7. Outline the events Paul discusses in verses 50-53.

8. In your own words, what does Paul mean by the quote in verses 54-55?

9. What practical difference is the hope of resurrection to have in the lives of people? (v. 58)

APPLY
Write out a prayer of thanks to the Lord for what the hope of the resurrection means to you.

Possibly the greatest verse in all of Scripture on hope is found in this passage. Photocopy this passage or write it out on a 3 × 5 card and put it on your dashboard or over the kitchen sink. Read this passage 7 times a day for 7 days until you have it stored away in your mind for the rest of your life.

"Therefore, my dear brothers, stand firm. Let nothing move you. Always give yourselves fully to the work of the Lord, because you know that your labor in the Lord is not in vain."
1 Corinthians 15:58 NIV

GROUP AGENDA

Divide into groups of 4 before you start to share. And follow the time recommendations.

TO BEGIN/10 Minutes (Choose 1 or 2)

☐ When you were a child, do you ever remember losing a pet? What did your parents tell you about a "heaven for pets"? ☐ Would you rather die in a hospital surrounded by pain-killing doctors or at home surrounded by family and friends? ☐ What person taught you a lot about the Christian life in the way that he/she died? ☐ What did you jot down for READ in your study?

TO GO DEEPER/20 Minutes (Choose 2 or 3)

☐ Go around and share the SEARCH portion of the Bible study. ☐ How does Paul explain to a rather uneducated and illiterate group of believers the profound truth of their own life

Continued on next page

For the trumpet will sound, the dead will be raised imperishable, and we will be changed. [53]For the perishable must clothe itself with the imperishable, and the mortal with immortality. [54]When the perishable has been clothed with the imperishable, and the mortal with immortality, then the saying that is written will come true: "Death has been swallowed up in victory."
[55]"Where, O death, is your victory?
    Where, O death, is your sting?"
[56]The sting of death is sin, and the power of sin is the law. [57]But thanks be to God! He gives us the victory through our Lord Jesus Christ.
[58]Therefore, my dear brothers, stand firm. Let nothing move you. Always give yourselves fully to the work of the Lord, because you know that your labor in the Lord is not in vain.

[a]45 Gen. 2:7 [b]49 Some early manuscripts *so let us* [c]54 Isaiah 25:8 [d]55 Hosea 13:14

113

NOTES ON 1 CORINTHIANS 15:35-38

Summary ... The false teachers in Corinth may be arguing against the future resurrection by asserting that it is absurd to imagine "the resuscitation of an immense number of corpses" (Barrett). The question is "foolish" (v. 36) when put that way; especially since it misses the whole point of the resurrection which is the transformation of the natural into the spiritual. Still, Paul must deal with the issue and so the subject of verses 35-58 is the nature of the resurrection body.

v. 35 ... This is the question the false teachers raise.

vv. 36-41 ... By means of two analogies (the seed and the body) Paul answers their

---

GROUP AGENDA continued

after death? ☐ How does the Christian view of life after death differ from those of other religions, such as the Hindu and the Moslem? ☐ What is the concept of heaven presented here? ☐ Case History: Six months after your friend lost her husband in a car accident, she suddenly turns bitter. "I hate God ... for letting this happen," she cries. She is a believer in Christ, but pretty weak right now. She calls on you at 3 o'clock in the morning. What do you say?

TO CLOSE/5-20 Minutes (Choose 1 or 2)

☐ Check out the memory verse to see if everyone has memorized it. Check to see if the verse meant anything special this week. ☐ What is the most comforting thing to you about the words of Paul here? What is the most encouraging? What fires you up? ☐ When, if ever, have you or a loved one been face-to-face with death? What did you learn from this experience? ☐ Read the prayers you wrote for APPLY as way of closing your meeting.

---

question and explains the nature of the resurrection body.

vv. 36-38 ... Death brings change (transformation), not extinction. Here Paul probes the nature of the transformation, his point being that what one plants is not what one gets in the end. A small grain of wheat grows mysteriously into a tall, grain-bearing stalk (John 12:24). So too our bodies will yield a quite new and glorious body after the resurrection.

vv. 39-41 ... A second analogy is used to show that, in fact, there are a host of different kinds of bodies and therefore it is not unreasonable to expect the resurrection body to be quite different from the natural body.

vv. 42-44a ... Paul reinforces the idea of verse 36: what is sown one way is raised in another. He makes this point by means of a series of antithetical comparisons: perishable/imperishable; dishonor/glory; weakness/power; natural/spiritual.

v. 42 **so will it be at the resurrection** ... i.e., "resurrection means transformation" (Barrett).

perishable ... literally, "corruption." This "is an evil power, by which the world is dominated in the old age (Romans 8:21). It affects not only human life, but the whole of creation. Its dominion will be ended in the age to come, at the beginning of which the resurrection takes place. Thus Paul's point is not simply that we shall have a new body, no longer subject to change and decay; but that new body will be appropriate to the new age ..." (Barrett).

v. 43 ... Paul now describes the nature of the changed body. The resurrection body is characterized by *glory* (brightness, radiance, splendor). This is a quality ascribed to God himself in which believers will somehow share (Philippians 3:21). The resurrection body will also be filled with *power*—another word often used to describe Christ.

v. 44 **natural/spiritual** ... Paul now defines the two kinds of bodies. The *natural* body is that which is animated by the soul (i.e., the natural life force) while the *spiritual* body has as its animating force the Holy Spirit. In verses 45-49 he will describe each body.

v. 44b ... here he reinforces verses 38-41: different bodies are appropriate to different circumstances. The resurrected body will not be simply a reanimated corpse. The natural body is mortal, and subject to death and decay. It is not appropriate to the New Age. The spiritual body, while having continuity with the natural body (which is the seed from which it springs) will be quite new and, in fact, will bear the marks of Christ's nature (v. 43).

vv. 45-49 ... Paul explains further the analogy of Adam and Christ (vv. 21-22), his point being (v. 49) that just as we shared the likeness of Adam's mortal body, we will share the likeness of Christ's spiritual body.

v. 48 ... The Christians, after their resurrection, will become a race of heavenly people.

v. 49 **The man from heaven** ... Jesus.

COMMENTS

vv. 50-58 . . . Paul concludes his argument for the resurrection of believers with a magnificent passage in which he points triumphantly to the future hope of the Christian.

v. 50 **flesh and blood** . . . i.e., living people cannot inherit the kingdom.

perishable . . . nor can the unchanged dead. What Paul is saying is that at the Second Coming neither the living nor the dead can take part in the kingdom without being changed.

v. 51 **mystery** . . . a truth about the End, once hidden but now revealed.

we . . . Paul expects to be alive at the Second Coming.

not all sleep . . . some Christians will be alive at the Second Coming.

all be changed . . . both the living and the dead will be changed.

v. 52 **in a flash** . . . this change will occur instantaneously.

the trumpet will sound . . . this transformation will occur at the Second Coming.

the dead will be raised . . . Those who are in the grave at the Second Coming will be transformed, as will the living.

v. 56 **The sting of death is sin** . . . "Considered genetically, the relationship means that sin is the cause of death; here it is considered empirically. Taking death as a given fact, sin is what embitters it, not only psychologically, in that it breeds remorse, but also theologically in that it makes clear that death is not merely a natural phenomenon, but a punishment, an evil that need not exist and would not exist if man were not in rebellion against his Creator" (Barrett).

v. 57 **victory** . . . In great joy, Paul exults in the fact that sin and law (that by which sin is made known) do not have the last word. Christ's death was a victory over sin and death.

v. 58 **my dear brothers** . . . his letter is at an end; his chastening is finished and so it is appropriate that he challenge them to allow this same Christ who has won victories for them to win victories through them.

your labor . . . is not in vain . . . because the resurrection is real, so the future is secure and magnificent.

Immortality
by Frederick Buechner

Immortal means death-proof. To believe in the immortality of the soul is to believe that though John Brown's body lies a-mouldering in the grave, his soul goes marching on simply because marching on is the nature of souls just the way producing apples is the nature of apple trees. Bodies die, but souls don't.

True or false, this is not the biblical view, although many who ought to know better assume it is. The biblical view differs in several significant ways:

1. As someone has put it, the biblical understanding of man is not that he has a body but that he is a body. When God made Adam, he did it by slapping some mud together to make a body and then breathing some breath into it to make a living soul. Thus the body and soul which make up a man are as inextricably part and parcel of each other as the leaves and flames that make up a bonfire. When you kick the bucket, you kick it one hundred percent. All of you. There is nothing left to go marching on with.

2. The idea that the body dies and the soul doesn't is an idea which implies that the body is something rather gross and embarrassing like a case of hemorrhoids. The Greeks spoke of it as the prison house of the soul. The suggestion was that to escape it altogether was something less than a disaster.

The Bible, on the other hand, sees the body in particular and the material world in general as a good and glorious invention. How could it be otherwise when it was invented by a good and glorious God?

3. Those who believe in the immortality of the soul believe that life after death is as natural a function of man as digestion after a meal.

The Bible instead speaks of resurrection. It is entirely unnatural. Man does not go on living beyond the grave because that's how he is made. Rather, he goes to his grave as dead as a doornail and is given his life back again by God (i.e., resurrected) just as he was given it by God in the first place, because that is the way God is made.

4. All the major Christian creeds affirm belief in resurrection *of the body*. In other words they affirm the belief that what God in spite of everything prizes enough to bring back to life is not just some disembodied echo of a human being but a new and revised version of all the things which made him the particular human being he was and which he needs something like a body to express: his personality, the way he looked, the sound of his voice.—Taken from *Wishful Thinking: A Theological ABC* (Harper and Row), pp. 41-43.

UNIT 27—The Collection/Requests/Final Greetings/1 Cor. 16:1-24

TEXT

The Collection for God's People

16 Now about the collection for God's people: Do what I told the Galatian churches to do. ²On the first day of every week, each one of you should set aside a sum of money in keeping with his income, saving it up, so that when I come no collections will have to be made. ³Then, when I arrive, I will give letters of introduction to the men you approve and send them with your gift to Jerusalem. ⁴If it seems advisable for me to go also, they will accompany me.

Personal Requests

⁵After I go through Macedonia, I will come to you—for I will be going through Macedonia. ⁶Perhaps I will stay with you awhile, or even spend the winter, so that you can help me on my journey, wherever I go. ⁷I do not want to see you now and make only a passing visit; I hope to spend some time with you, if the Lord permits. ⁸But I will stay on at Ephesus until Pentecost, ⁹because a great door for effective work has opened to me, and there are many who oppose me.

¹⁰If Timothy comes, see to it that he has nothing to fear while he is with you, for he is carrying on the work of the Lord, just as I am. ¹¹No one, then, should refuse to accept him. Send him on his way in peace so that he may return to me. I am expecting him along with the brothers.

¹²Now about our brother Apollos: I strongly urged him to go to you with the brothers. He was quite unwilling to go now, but he will go when he has the opportunity. ¹³Be on your guard; stand firm in the faith; be men of courage; be strong. ¹⁴Do everything in love.

¹⁵You know that the household of Stephanas were the first converts in Achaia, and they have devoted themselves to the service of the saints. I urge you, brothers, ¹⁶to submit to such as

Continued on next page

STUDY

READ

First Reading/First Impressions
How would you feel if, like Timothy, Paul was sending you to this church?

Second Reading/Big Idea
What "tone of voice" do you pick up as Paul concludes his letter to such a difficult church?

SEARCH

1. From Acts 11:30, 24:17, Romans 15:25-28, and 2 Corinthians 8:13-14, what can you learn about this collection Paul was making among the Greek churches?

2. How would you explain his principle about how much to give (v. 2) to a friend?

3. What is significant about who will have the accountability and responsibility over this gift? (vv. 3-4)

4. Although Paul wants to come, he will delay for a while. As Timothy and Apollos plan to do so soon, what fears or hesitations might they have? (See also 1:12; 3:5.)

5. How do Stephanas and the others (vv. 15-18) model the way the Corinthians ought to live?

6. How do you account for the warmth of verses 19-24, given all the hard things Paul wrote to this church?

APPLY
Take each of Paul's concluding exhortations in verses 13-14 and write out what each one means specifically for you at this time.

Be on your guard:

Stand firm in your faith:

Have courage:

Be strong:

Do everything in love:

Since this is the last session in this course, take a moment and recall these highlights:

WHAT WAS THE HIGH POINT IN THE COURSE?

WHAT WAS THE GREATEST TRUTH YOU LEARNED?

WHAT DO YOU APPRECIATE MOST ABOUT THE GROUP YOU WERE IN?

WHAT IS THE BIGGEST CHALLENGE YOU FACE RIGHT NOW?

WHAT ARE YOU GOING TO DO ABOUT IT?

GROUP AGENDA

Divide into groups of 4 before you start to share. And follow the time recommendations.

TO BEGIN / 10 Minutes (Choose 1 or 2)

☐ What is the best trip you ever took with your family when you were a child? What was it that made this trip so special? ☐ When, if ever, has a person given you money when you really needed it? How did it make you feel? ☐ If you had to send someone on business to take your place, who would be one of the best representatives you could send? ☐ What did you jot down for READ?

TO GO DEEPER / 20 Minutes (Choose 2 or 3)

☐ Share the SEARCH of the Bible study, one question at a time. ☐ What are the major topics that Paul deals with in this chapter? ☐ What is

Continued on next page

---

these and to everyone who joins in the work, and labors at it. [17]I was glad when Stephanas, Fortunatus and Achaicus arrived, because they have supplied what was lacking from you. [18]For they refreshed my spirit and yours also. Such men deserve recognition.

Final Greetings
[19]The churches in the province of Asia send you greetings. Aquila and Priscilla greet you warmly in the Lord, and so does the church that meets at their house. [20]All the brothers here send you greetings. Greet one another with a holy kiss.
[21]I, Paul, write this greeting in my own hand.
[22]If anyone does not love the Lord—a curse be on him. Come, O Lord.!
[23]The grace of the Lord Jesus be with you.
[24]My love to all of you in Christ Jesus.

[a]19 Greek *Prisca*, a variant of *Priscilla* [b]22 In Aramaic the expression *Come, O Lord* is *Marana tha*

NOTES ON 1 CORINTHIANS 16:1-24

Summary... Paul ends his epistle by attending to a series of "housekeeping matters": the collection for the poor in Jerusalem; his own travel plans and those of his colleagues; the question of Stephanas' ministry in the church; and greetings from various friends.

v. 1 **Now about**... Paul deals with yet another question which they asked in their letter (7:1; 8:1; 12:1).

the collection... When in Jerusalem, Paul had agreed to help support the poor there (Galatians 2:10). (See also Acts 11:29-30; 24:17; Romans 15:25-28; 2 Corinthians 8, 9.) In this way the Gentile and the Jewish wings of the church would be bound together in a new fashion. Although this collection bears a superficial resemblance to the temple tax required of all Jews and paid at Jerusalem, what Paul suggests is different in that this is a voluntary collection given to the mother church in Jerusalem in order to aid the poor there.

v. 2 **On the first day**... Sunday, when Christians met for worship.

set aside... Paul is not calling for a collection to be taken each Sunday for his purpose. Rather he asks individual Christians to set aside funds on their own.

no collections will have to be made... Paul hoped that each person would have a sum of money set aside, ready to hand over when he came so that he would not have to bother about the time-consuming process of taking a collection.

v. 3 **letters of introduction**... a common way by which a person was commended to another person or community.

men you approve... The Corinthians, not Paul, would select their own team of messengers, so as to defuse any possible misunderstanding about *why* Paul was taking up the collection and how it would be used.

v. 4 ... Acts 20:1-21:17 describes a journey by Paul from Greece to Jerusalem and although no Corinthians are named directly as traveling companions, it seems likely on the basis of Romans 15:26 (in which he notes the success of the Corinthian collection) that this was so.

vv. 5-9 Paul now describes his further travel plans. He is writing from Ephesus (v. 8), where he plans to stay a while since he is having a fruitful ministry there. When he does leave, he will come across the Aegean Sea to Macedonia (possibly going to Thessalonica). From Macedonia his intention is to travel south to Athens or Corinth.

vv. 10-11 ... Paul next mentions Timothy's plans. Timothy's trip to Corinth is somewhat in doubt ("*If* Timothy comes"... v. 10). Why Timothy is afraid is not clear. Perhaps as Paul's assistant he may fear a hostile welcome from the unpredictable Corinthians.

vv. 12 ... The Corinthians evidently want a visit from Apollos. Paul informs them that Apollos is not willing to visit them yet. Perhaps he and Paul have decided that since one "party" is rallying around his name, the cause of unity would be aided if he did *not* visit.

Now about... They may have asked about Apollos in their letter.

v. 13 **Be on your guard**... This word is often used to urge watchfulness in terms of the Second Coming. "Be alert to the events of the last days, lest they catch you unaware," seems to be Paul's admonition.

v. 14 ... In chapter 13 Paul has defined this way of love for them.

vv. 15-16 ... Paul calls upon the Corinthians to recognize the ministry of Stephanas and his family. These people have given themselves over to the service of others. Furthermore, Paul calls upon the

---

GROUP AGENDA continued

the teaching on tithing or church-giving here? How does this differ from the Old Testament? ☐ If you had been in the church in Corinth and were guilty of some of the misbehavior that he has addressed in this letter, how would you feel about his plan to visit you ... "even spend the winter"? ☐ Case History: Your friend lives in a modern-day "Sodom and Gomorrah" kind of city like Corinth. The church there is as bad as the culture. Your friend is messed up in some of this "worldliness." What is your advice for your friend? For his church?

TO CLOSE/5-20 Minutes (Choose 1 or 2)

☐ What did you jot down for APPLY? ☐ What situation in your life right now is calling for you to exhibit the greatest amount of courage? (v. 13) Of strength? Of firmness? ☐ What was the high point in this course for you? What is the most important lesson you have learned? ☐ What have you appreciated the most about the group you have been in? ☐ What is the next step for you in your own spiritual journey?

COMMENTS

Corinthians to subordinate themselves to these their natural leaders—no doubt a most difficult request for the stubborn, proud Corinthians.

v. 16 **and to everyone who joins in the work** ... in fact, it is not just to the family of Stephanas that the Corinthians should look for leadership. Other emerged leaders ought also to be followed in a spirit of submission for the sake of ministry in general.

v. 17 ... These three supplied Paul with some of the information he has about the Corinthian Church. While Stephanas is also presumably mentioned in verse 15, this seems to be the only reference to Fortunatus and Achaicus.

v. 18 **recognition** ... Here are more of the natural leaders in the church (who presumably have the potential for bringing order out of the chaos in Corinth if they are allowed to do so by the rest of the church).

v. 19 **Aquila and Priscilla** ... They are now, apparently, in Ephesus. Paul met them first in Corinth where they journeyed after Jews were expelled from Rome. Aquila and Priscilla were, presumably, quite wealthy since they were business people; they traveled freely; and they had a house in Ephesus—where the (or "a") church met.

v. 20 **a holy kiss** ... This was a custom used in the early church as part of the worship service. Kisses were a common form of greeting in biblical times. In the parable of the prodigal son, the father embraces and kisses his returned son (Luke 15:20). The Ephesian elders wept when Paul left, embracing and kissing him (Acts 20:37). See also Romans 16:16; 2 Corinthians 13:12; 1 Thessalonians 5:26; 1 Peter 5:14.

v. 21 ... Paul normally dictated his letters and then authenticated them by writing a final comment in his own handwriting.

v. 22 **Come, O Lord** ... This is an Aramaic expression, *Marana tha* transliterated by Paul into Greek (see also Revelation 22:20). In *The Didache,* an early Christian worship manual, this same phrase is used during the Communion service. When the Lord returns this would mark the moment that a *curse* was effected upon those who had refused to love the Lord.

vv. 23-24 He concludes his letter in typical fashion. Paul began (1:1-9) by thanking God for the Corinthians and he ends his letter in the same spirit. They are beloved brothers and sisters in the Lord despite all the hard things he has had to say to them. In fact, it is because he loved them that he wrote what he did.

Giving—Gift or Role?
by Peter Wagner

The way Christian roles operate alongside spiritual gifts is vividly illustrated by the gift of giving.

There is no question that every Christian is to give part of his or her income to the Lord. According to the Bible, every person should set definite giving goals and give with cheerfulness (see 2 Corinthians 9:7). This is a Christian role, and there are no exceptions. Rich Christians should give and poor Christians should give. Young marrieds who have low incomes and high expenses should give alongside more mature people who are financially secure. New Christians should be taught to give as soon as they begin growing in their faith.

How much should Christians give?

As I read the Scriptures, I have to conclude that a tithe, meaning 10 percent of one's income off the top, is the bare minimum for exercising the role of giving. I am not ordinarily legalistic in my views of Christian behavior, but I have to say that I believe that anyone who is under the 10 percent figure is engaging in a form of spiritual cheating. Some cheat the I.R.S. regularly and get away with it. No one cheats God and gets away with it. "Be not deceived; God is not mocked; for whatsoever a man soweth, that shall he also reap" (Galatians 6:7).

It is a well-known fact that a large number of Christians are not exercising their role of giving. The average giving for Christians in America is something around $145 per year. The average salary is considerably more than $1,450. My church, Lake Avenue Congregational Church, is a fairly affluent church, basically upper-middle class. However I once figured that if all our members received California welfare payments and tithed, our income would go up by 40 percent!... —Taken from *Your Spiritual Gifts Can Help Your Church Grow* (Regal Books), pp. 92-93, 95-96.